MAGIC HOUSE
OF NUMBERS

Books by Irving Adler

Magic House

of

Numbers

IRVING ADLER

Illustrated by
RUTH ADLER

THE JOHN DAY COMPANY
NEW YORK

Contents

MAGIC HOUSE
OF NUMBERS

CHAPTER I

Number Curiosities

Tools and Toys

NUMBERS are tools with which we work. The carpenter uses numbers as well as a saw to cut a piece of lumber to the right size. The grocer uses numbers as well as a scale to weigh out the food he sells. The accountant and the plumber, the engineer and the farmer, the scientist and the salesman all use numbers to help them at their jobs.

But numbers are also toys with which we can play. We can use them to solve fascinating puzzles, do mystifying tricks, and play exciting games. This book introduces you to some of the many ways in which you can have fun with numbers.

Mysterious Steps

You may have read stories about a magic house that is full of surprises. Trap doors in the floor hide secret steps that lead to mysterious caves under the ground. Sliding panels in the wall hide other steps that lead to curious attics, or even a strange new world. The house of numbers is such a magic house. It has hidden steps behind a secret door. These steps will lead us, first, to some strange numbers as interesting as people in a circus side show. Then they will lead us into a curious world of numbers different from our own.

9

To find the hidden steps in the house of numbers, let us look first at the ordinary steps that are out in the open. We use them when we want to climb up to higher and higher numbers. We can climb slowly by counting by ones: 1, 2, 3, 4, 5, 6, 7, and so on. Counting by ones is like a local train on a railroad. It stops at every station. We can climb up faster by counting by twos, or threes, or fours, or by any other number. This gives us the multiplication tables. Counting by twos gives us the "two-times" table. Counting by threes gives us the "three-times" table, and so on. The multiplication tables are like express trains on a railroad. They skip some stations, and stop at others. The numbers we stop at when we count by twos, like 2, 4, 6, 8, and so on, are called *even* numbers. They can all be divided by 2, without any remainder. The numbers we skip when we count by twos, like 1, 3, 5, 7, and so on, are called *odd* numbers. When you divide one of them by 2, there is always a remainder of 1.

As we climb up the steps, the first numbers we meet are numbers that are written down with a single figure. Each of these numbers, from *one* to *nine*, has a figure all its own. *Zero*, the ground floor from which we climb, also has its own figure. These separate figures are called *digits*. There are ten of them: 0, 1, 2, 3, 4, 5, 6, 7, 8, and 9. But when we go above the number *nine*, we begin meeting numbers that are written down with more than one figure. The number *ten* is written with two digits, a 1 followed by a 0. The number *thirty-six* is written with two digits, a 3 followed by a 6.

Every number with more than one digit has a secret door which leads to some hidden steps. We can open the door by *adding up the digits*. Let us do it with the numbers we get when we count by ones, and with each of the multiplication tables, to see what the hidden steps are like. If the number is 14, we add the 1 and 4 to get 5. If the number is 28, we add the 2 and 8 to get 10. But this result has two digits, 1 and 0. So we add them, too, to get 1. In this way we finally get a single digit hidden behind each number.

COUNTING BY ONES

The open steps	The hidden steps
1	1
2	2
3	3
4	4
5	5
6	6
7	7
8	8
9	9
10	1
11	2
12	3
13	4
14	5
15	6
16	7
17	8
18	9

Here the hidden steps are made up of the numbers from 1 to 9, repeated over and over again.

Counting by Twos (The "Two-Times" Table)

	The open steps	The hidden steps
2 × 1	2	2
2 × 2	4	4
2 × 3	6	6
2 × 4	8	8
2 × 5	10	1
2 × 6	12	3
2 × 7	14	5
2 × 8	16	7
2 × 9	18	9
2 × 10	20	2
2 × 11	22	4
2 × 12	24	6
2 × 13	26	8
2 × 14	28	1
2 × 15	30	3
2 × 16	32	5
2 × 17	34	7
2 × 18	36	9

Notice how the hidden steps in the "two-times" table are arranged in groups. In the first group they go up two numbers at a time, like the open steps, stopping at even numbers only. In the second group they go up two numbers at a time, stopping at the odd numbers only. Then these two groups are repeated over and over again.

In the "three-times" table, the hidden steps have only one short group of steps, the numbers 3, 6, and 9, repeated over and over again:

COUNTING BY THREES (THE "THREE-TIMES" TABLE)

	The open steps	The hidden steps
3 × 1	3	3
3 × 2	6	6
3 × 3	9	9
3 × 4	12	3
3 × 5	15	6
3 × 6	18	9
3 × 7	21	3
3 × 8	24	6
3 × 9	27	9
3 × 10	30	3
3 × 11	33	6
3 × 12	36	9

There is a surprise in the hidden steps of the "four-times" table. At first they do not look like steps at all, but like a disorderly jumble of numbers. But if you look closely, you see that there are two sets of steps that are interlocked, with a step of one set between every two steps of the other. And this time, the steps go down instead of up, and without skipping any numbers. In the table below, the two sets of hidden steps are printed in separate columns, to make it easier to recognize them.

13

Counting by Fours (The "Four-Times" Table)

	The open steps	The hidden steps
4 × 1	4	4
4 × 2	8	8
4 × 3	12	3
4 × 4	16	7
4 × 5	20	2
4 × 6	24	6
4 × 7	28	1
4 × 8	32	5
4 × 9	36	9
4 × 10	40	4
4 × 11	44	8
4 × 12	48	3
4 × 13	52	7
4 × 14	56	2
4 × 15	60	6
4 × 16	64	1

The hidden steps in the "five-times" table also have two sets of steps that are interlocked. Here the steps go up instead of down:

Counting by Fives (The "Five-Times" Table)

	The open steps	The hidden steps
5 × 1	5	5
5 × 2	10	1
5 × 3	15	6
5 × 4	20	2
5 × 5	25	7
5 × 6	30	3
5 × 7	35	8
5 × 8	40	4
5 × 9	45	9
5 × 10	50	5
5 × 11	55	1
5 × 12	60	6
5 × 13	65	2
5 × 14	70	7
5 × 15	75	3
5 × 16	80	8
5 × 17	85	4
5 × 18	90	9

The hidden steps in the "six-times" table are like those in the "three-times" table, but they go in the opposite direction, as shown in the Table on the next page.

Counting by Sixes (The "Six-Times" Table)

	The open steps	The hidden steps
6 × 1	6	6
6 × 2	12	3
6 × 3	18	9
6 × 4	24	6
6 × 5	30	3
6 × 6	36	9
6 × 7	42	6
6 × 8	48	3

The hidden steps in the "seven-times" table are like those in the "two-times" table, but they go in the opposite direction:

Counting by Sevens (The "Seven-Times" Table)

	The open steps	The hidden steps
7 × 1	7	7
7 × 2	14	5
7 × 3	21	3
7 × 4	28	1
7 × 5	35	8
7 × 6	42	6
7 × 7	49	4
7 × 8	56	2
7 × 9	63	9
7 × 10	70	7
7 × 11	77	5
7 × 12	84	3
7 × 13	91	1

The hidden steps in the "eight-times" table are the opposite of those we got from counting by ones:

COUNTING BY EIGHTS (THE "EIGHT-TIMES" TABLE)

	The open steps	The hidden steps
8 × 1	8	8
8 × 2	16	7
8 × 3	24	6
8 × 4	32	5
8 × 5	40	4
8 × 6	48	3
8 × 7	56	2
8 × 8	64	1
8 × 9	72	9
8 × 10	80	8

The hidden steps in the "nine-times" table are the strangest of all. They don't go anywhere. They don't go up and they don't go down:

COUNTING BY NINES (THE "NINE-TIMES" TABLE)

	The open steps	The hidden steps
9 × 1	9	9
9 × 2	18	9
9 × 3	27	9
9 × 4	36	9
9 × 5	45	9
9 × 6	54	9
9 × 7	63	9
9 × 8	72	9
9 × 9	81	9

The Key to the Hidden Steps

The hidden steps in the "nine-times" table are the only ones that don't go up or down. They stay in one place, at the number 9. This shows that there is something special about the number 9. The other tables also point to the number 9 as a special kind of number, when we notice which tables had the same kind of hidden steps going in opposite directions. We found four kinds of steps, and they divide the numbers from 1 to 8 into four pairs in this way:

KIND OF STEPS	COUNTING BY	
Up one at a time	ones	
Down one at a time	eights	But $1 + 8 = 9$.
Odds and evens up	twos	
Odds and evens down	sevens	But $2 + 7 = 9$.
Up three at a time	threes	
Down three at a time	sixes	But $3 + 6 = 9$.
Interlocked, down	fours	
Interlocked, up	fives	But $4 + 5 = 9$.

The number 9 is the key to the secret of the hidden steps. We can discover the secret by using the number 9 as a divisor of all the numbers in the open steps of the tables. Suppose we divide 13 by 9. The 9 goes into 13 once, and *there is a remainder of 4.* But 4 is the hidden step we got by adding the digits 1 and 3. If we divide 17 by 9, *the remainder is 8.* But 1 plus 7 is also 8. Try this with any number, and you will see that *the sum of the digits of a number is always equal to the remainder you get when you divide that number by 9.* The hidden steps in the multiplication tables are the remainders left over when we divide the numbers in the open steps by 9. The numbers in the "nine-times" table look like exceptions to this rule, but they really aren't. If we divide a number like 27 by 9, we usually say that it goes three times, with a remainder of 0. But we might also say that it goes twice, with a remainder of 9. So the hidden steps in the "nine-times" table, too, are remainders left over after we divide by 9.

Casting Out Nines

Dividing is a short cut for subtracting the same number over and over again. When we divide 33 by 9, it goes three times, and there is a remainder of 6. This means that if we start with 33, and take away 9 over and over again, after three subtractions we would end up with 6:

$$33 - 9 = 24; \quad 24 - 9 = 15; \quad 15 - 9 = 6.$$

Because we get the remainder by taking away nines, finding this remainder is called *casting out nines*. Repeated subtraction is one way of doing it. Division is a shorter way of doing it. But adding the digits is the shortest way of all, as you can see in the example below, where we cast out nines from 52:

REPEATED SUBTRACTION:	DIVISION:	ADDING DIGITS:
52	5	$5 + 2 = 7$
$-\ 9$	$9\overline{)52}$	
43	45	
$-\ 9$	7 (remainder)	
34		
$-\ 9$		
25		
$-\ 9$		
16		
$-\ 9$		
7 (remainder)		

Checking Your Addition

The last two examples showed that 33 is made up of 3 nines and a 6, and 52 is made up of 5 nines and a 7. Suppose we wanted to add 33 and 52. We could write the example in the two ways shown below:

33	3 nines and 6
+ 52	5 nines and 7
85	8 nines and 13

Doing the example the first way, the answer is 85. Now, if we cast out nines, the remainder is 4, because 85 is made up of 9 nines and 4. Doing the example the second way, the answer is 8 nines and 13. But 13 has another nine in it, and a remainder of 4. So casting out nines from 13 gives the same remainder as casting out nines from 85. This shows that you get the same remainder whether you add first, and then cast out nines, or cast out nines first, and then add. This fact gives us a simple way of checking answers to examples in addition: Cast out nines from each number to be added. Then add all the remainders, and cast out nines if necessary. The result should be the same as the remainder you get when you cast nines out of the answer. If it isn't the same, then you know the answer is wrong. The method is shown in two examples below. In the first one, the addition was done correctly. In the second one there is a mistake in the addition, and casting out nines warns us of the mistake.

EXAMPLE I:

153	$1 + 5 + 3 =$	9	
27	$2 + 7 =$	9	The remainders
345	$3 + 4 + 5 =$	12	agree when there
86	$8 + 6 =$	14	is no mistake.
611		44	

$$6 + 1 + 1 = 8 \qquad 4 + 4 = 8$$

20

EXAMPLE II: 427 $4 + 2 + 7 = 13$

                51     $5 + 1 = 6$ The remainders

               113     $1 + 1 + 3 = 5$ do not agree, so

               ───   ──   there is a mis-

               581   24   take.

     $5 + 8 + 1 = 14$ $2 + 4 = 6$

         $1 + 4 = 5$

If the second example is done correctly, the answer is 591. Then, $5 + 9 + 1 = 15$, and if we add the digits of 15, $1 + 5 = 6$. Now the remainders agree, as they should.

Casting out nines is not a foolproof check. It uncovers errors only if the error is not a multiple of nine. If, in example II, we got the wrong answer 501 (90 less than the right answer), the sum of the digits would be 6, and it would seem to check even though the answer is wrong. But this kind of mistake would be rare. When you cast out nines, if the remainders do not agree, the answer is *surely wrong*. If the remainders do agree, the answer is *probably right*.

The Secret of the Hidden Steps

Now we can understand why the hidden steps go up or down the way they do. In the "two-times" table, we are counting by twos, so the open steps go up two at a time. The first four numbers in the open steps are less than nine. So when we divide each of them by nine, the quotient is 0, and the entire number is the remainder. That is why the same four numbers appear in the hidden steps. The fifth number in the open steps is 10. Its remainder, when we divide by nine, is 1. The next numbers in the open steps continue to go up two at a time, so their remainders go up two at a time, too. That is why the next hidden steps after 1 are 3, 5, 7, and 9. Continuing to go up two at a time, the next number would be 11. But 11 has a nine in it that we can cast out, leaving a remainder of 2. That is why

21

the hidden steps now start all over again with the numbers 2, 4, 6, 8.

To understand the "eight-times" table, let us notice first another fact about casting out nines. There are two ways of recognizing the remainder that is left when we divide a number by nine. One way is to see how high it is above the multiple of nine that is just below it. For example, the number 25 is 7 above 18. That is why the remainder is 7 when we divide 25 by 9. The other way is to see how far the number is below the next multiple of nine above it. For example, the number 25 is 2 below 27. Then, if we take 2 from 9, we know the remainder is 7. The number 33 is 3 below 36. Take 3 from 9, and we know the remainder is 6. Now let's apply this knowledge to the "eight-times" table, where the open steps start with 8, and go up 8 at a time. The first of the steps is 8, which is 1 below a multiple of 9. So the next step is 2 below a multiple of nine. That is why the remainder is 7. The next step is 3 below a multiple of 9, so the remainder is 6. The amount that the steps are below a multiple of nine increases by 1 at a time. That is why the remainders decrease by 1 at a time.

In the "four-times" table, the numbers in the open steps go up 4 at a time. If we go up the steps *two steps at a time* by skipping every other step, then the increase is 8 at a time. But, as we just saw in the "eight-times" table, when numbers increase by 8 at a time, their remainders decrease by 1 at a time, because 8 is 1 less than 9. That is why, if we start with the first of the hidden steps and then skip every other step, we get a series of numbers that go down 1 at a time. If we start with the second step and then skip every other step, we get the other series of numbers going down 1 at a time. This explains why the hidden steps are made up of two sets of steps that are interlocked.

Now that you know the secret, try to explain the hidden

steps in the other tables by yourself. Then you can see if you explained them correctly by looking up Answer No. 1 in the answer section in the back of this book.

Checking Multiplication

You can use casting out nines to check multiplication examples, too. First get the remainders of the two multipliers. Then multiply them, and cast out nines if necessary. The result will agree with the remainder of your answer, if the answer is right. The method is shown in two examples below:

EXAMPLE I:

$$
\begin{array}{r}
116 \\
\times\ 23 \\
\hline
348 \\
232 \\
\hline
2668
\end{array}
\qquad
\begin{array}{r}
1 + 1 + 6 = 8 \\
2 + 3 = 5 \\
\hline
40 \\
4 + 0 = 4
\end{array}
$$

The remainders agree when there is no mistake.

$2 + 6 + 6 + 8 = 22;\quad 2 + 2 = 4$

EXAMPLE II:

$$
\begin{array}{r}
137 \\
\times\ 26 \\
\hline
825 \\
274 \\
\hline
3565
\end{array}
\qquad
\begin{array}{r}
1 + 3 + 7 = 11 \\
2 + 6 = 8 \\
\hline
88 \\
8 + 8 = 16 \\
1 + 6 = 7
\end{array}
$$

The remainders do not agree, so there is a mistake.

$3 + 5 + 6 + 5 = 19$
$1 + 9 = 10;\quad 1 + 0 = 1$

The Printing-Press Number

There are some strange numbers lurking in the multiplication tables. One of them is the number 12,345,679. It behaves like a printing press. If you want a digit from 1 to 9, it will print a lot of them for you. For example, suppose you want some 1's. Then multiply the number by 1×9:

$$
\begin{array}{r}
12345679 \\
\times \qquad 9 \\
\hline
111111111
\end{array}
$$

If you want 2's, then multiply by 2×9:

$$
\begin{array}{r}
12345679 \\
\times \qquad 18 \\
\hline
98765432 \\
12345679 \\
\hline
222222222
\end{array}
$$

If you want 3's, then multiply by 3×9, or 27.

$$
\begin{array}{r}
12345679 \\
\times \qquad 27 \\
\hline
86419753 \\
24691358 \\
\hline
333333333
\end{array}
$$

To get 4's, multiply by 36. To get 5's, multiply by 45. To get 6's, multiply by 54. To get 7's, multiply by 63. To get 8's, multiply by 72. To get 9's, multiply by 81.

The strange behavior of this number is explained by casting out nines. We know that the sum of the digits of a number tells us what the remainder is when we divide the number by nine. The number 111,111,111 has nine digits, and they are all ones. So the sum of its digits is 9. This tells us that if we divide the number by nine, the answer comes

24

out a whole number. That number is 12,345,679. Naturally, if we multiply this by nine, we get the 111,111,111 back again. If we multiply by 2×9, since the multiplier is twice as large, the answer comes out twice as large: $2 \times 111,111,$-111 is 222,222,222. If we multiply by 3×9, since the multiplier is three times as large, the answer comes out three times as large: $3 \times 111,111,111$ is 333,333,333. If we multiply by 4×9, the answer comes out four times as large, and so on.

The Number that Plays Ring-Around-a-Rosy

Another strange number in the multiplication tables is the number 142,857. Arrange the digits in this number in a circle, as shown in the diagram, so that the last figure 7, is written just before the first figure, 1. Now multiply 142,857 by each of the numbers 2, 3, 4, 5, 6.

142857	142857	142857	142857	142857
× 2	× 3	× 4	× 5	× 6
285714	428571	571428	714285	857142

All the answers are made up of the digits of 142,857 in a new arrangement. Each arrangement is one we can get by moving the digits around the circle, so that we allow each digit in turn to take the place of 1 and serve as the first digit of the number. Multiplying the number 142,857 by 2, 3, 4, 5, or 6 makes it play ring-around-a-rosy.

Now try multiplying 142,857 by 7. The result will be a pleasant surprise.

CHAPTER II

The Dresses that Numbers Wear

THE number 9 is the key to the secret of the hidden steps, because adding the digits of a number is like casting out nines. But this is true only because of the special way in which we write numbers. Our written numbers are based on a clever system we got from the Arabs which permits us to write an unlimited amount of numbers with only a limited amount of digits. This system grew out of an ancient method of calculating with the help of pebbles. In fact, the word calculate comes from the Latin word *calculus,* meaning pebble. Let us retrace the steps by which pebble reckoning led to our modern numbers.

If a bookkeeper in ancient times had to add the numbers 7, 5, and 8, he could do it easily by first counting out seven pebbles, then five more pebbles, and then eight more pebbles. Then he could count how many pebbles he had altogether. But if he had a lot of numbers to add, or big numbers to add, he would end up with a tremendous number of pebbles to count. People found after a while that it was easier to count a big pile of pebbles if they counted out small piles with ten pebbles in each pile. Then all they had to do was count how many tens they had plus any pebbles left over. For example, adding 7, 5, and 8 leads to two piles of ten pebbles each. Adding 9, 6, 8, and 9 leads to three piles of ten pebbles each and two pebbles left over. But they still found it inconvenient to have large numbers of pebbles on the counting table. Then somebody got a bright idea. He thought of a way of replacing a whole pile of ten pebbles by one single pebble. But, of course, he had to do it in such a way that he could tell that this single pebble stood for ten, and not for one. We do something like that today in our money system. When we have ten pennies, we can exchange them for one dime. We can tell when a single coin stands for ten cents instead of one cent because it is a *different kind* of coin. We also do the same sort of thing when we use poker chips to keep score in a game. When we have ten chips that are worth one point each, we can exchange them for one chip of another color. We can tell when a single chip stands for ten points instead of one point because it has a *different color*. But the ancient book-keepers had an even simpler idea. To show that a pebble stood for ten, they didn't use a pebble of a different kind or of a different color. They merely put the pebble in a *different place*. They had their counting tables divided into columns. Pebbles that stood for one each were put into the column on the extreme right. Pebbles that stood for ten each were put into the second column from the right. With this scheme, it was never necessary to have more than nine pebbles in the first column. As soon as they had ten pebbles in the first column, they could remove them, and put one pebble into the second column to take their place. Then, to avoid having too many pebbles in the second column, they extended the system. As soon as they had ten pebbles in the second column, they removed them and put one pebble into the third column to take their place. A pebble in the third column stood for ten tens, or one hundred. In the same way, a pebble in the fourth column stood for ten hundreds, or one thousand, and so on.

After a calculation was finished, the result had to be written down. The picture opposite shows pebbles arranged on a counting table. To show the number that they stand for, a Roman bookkeeper would have written CXI. He used I to stand for the pebble in the first column on his right because the I, like the pebble there, stood for *one*. He used X to stand for the pebble in the second column, because the X, like the pebble there, stood for *ten*. He used C to stand for the pebble in the third column, because the C, like the pebble there, stood for *one hundred.*

He used a different symbol for every column to show that the pebbles in different columns stood for different numbers. But the Arabian bookkeepers decided that this was unnecessary. They said, "We use the *same pebbles* to stand for *different numbers* by putting them into *different columns*. So we can use the *same symbols* to stand for *different numbers*, by putting *them* into *different columns*, too." Since their symbol for the number *one* was 1, they wrote the number shown by the pebbles on the counting table as 111. The symbols are arranged in columns the way the pebbles are. The figure in the first column on the right, like the pebble in the first column, stands for *one*. The symbol in the second column, like the pebble in the second column, stands for *ten*. The symbol in the third column, like the pebble in the third column, stands for *one hundred*.

In this system, they didn't need different symbols for the different columns, but they did need different symbols to show how many pebbles there are in one column. A column might have any number of pebbles from one to nine. To show these numbers they used the symbols 1, 2, 3, 4, 5, 6, 7, 8, and 9. To show that a column was empty, they used the symbol 0, which they had learned from the people of India. That is how we got our present system of writing numbers. The number 9 is a very special number in this system because it is the highest number for which a separate symbol had to be used. No new symbol is needed to show the number ten, because we show it by putting a 1 into the second column. When we write 10, it means 1 group of ten plus 0. When we write 11, it means 1 group of ten plus 1. When we write 21, it means 2 groups of ten plus 1.

If We Had Eight Fingers

In our system of writing numbers, a 1 in the second column stands for ten, because in ancient times people had formed the habit of counting things in groups of ten. It was natural for them to put ten things into a group because they counted on their fingers. But suppose human hands had been different with only four fingers on each hand. Then they would have counted things in groups of eight instead. When they reckoned with pebbles, as soon as they had *eight* pebbles in the first column on the right, they would have removed them, and put one pebble into the second column to take their place. In that case the Arabian scheme for writing numbers would have come out different.

If our number system were based on groups of eight instead of ten, here is how numbers would be written: We

30

would still need separate symbols for the numbers from zero to seven, so we could write them as 0, 1, 2, 3, 4, 5, 6, and 7. But we would not need a separate symbol for eight, because eight makes a group, and we would show a group of eight by putting a 1 into the second column from the right. Then 10 would mean 1 group of eight plus 0, or *eight*. The written number 11 would mean 1 group of eight plus 1, or *nine*. The written symbol 21 would mean 2 groups of eight plus 1, or *seventeen*. A number system like this, based on groups of eight, is called an eight-scale. The number system based on groups of ten is called a ten-scale.

In the ten-scale, a 1 in the third column from the right means ten times ten, or a hundred. In the eight scale it would mean eight times eight, or sixty-four. In the same way, a 1 in the fourth column would mean eight times eight times eight, or five hundred twelve.

A Number Can Change Its Dress

What number does 312 stand for? We can't simply say that it stands for three hundred twelve, because that is true only in the ten-scale. In the eight-scale it stands for a different number. In the eight-scale it stands for 3 sixty-fours plus 1 eight plus 2, or two hundred two. In other words, 312 in the eight-scale means 202 in the ten-scale. The same number has to be written in different ways when we use different scales. The written number is like a dress that the actual number wears when it appears in public. The scale is like the style of the dress. When we change the scale, the number changes its dress.

We are all used to reading numbers in the ten-scale. Let's learn how to recognize them even when they are dressed in the style of the eight-scale. Remember, to keep from being confused, the difference between numbers written out in words, and numbers written in digits. The numbers written in words are always the same; the numbers written in digits will be different depending on what scale they are in. For instance, *seventeen* is always *seventeen*. But 17 is *seventeen* in the ten-scale but only *fifteen* in the eight-scale.

Now look at the numbers below, written in the eight-scale. How would the same numbers be written in the ten-scale?

23   104   36   215   64   420

Let's do the first two together for practice. The number 23 means 2 eights plus 3, or nineteen, which in the ten-scale we write 19. The number 104 means 1 sixty-four plus no eights plus four, which in the ten-scale would be 64 plus 4, or 68. Now try the others yourself. You will find the answers in the answer section. (Answer No. 2)

Casting Out Sevens

In the eight-scale, the highest number that has a symbol of its own is *seven*. So the number seven would play the same special part in this scale that the number nine plays in the ten-scale. Then adding the digits of a number would be like casting out *sevens* instead of nines. For example, in the eight-scale, the number seventeen is written as 21. Adding the digits gives us 3, and 3 is the remainder when we divide seventeen by seven.

Eight-Scale Arithmetic

In a number system based on groups of eight, the addition and multiplication tables would be different compared to those we use today. We would still say $1 + 1 = 2$, and $2 + 2 = 4$, but $4 + 4$ would be 10, because 10 would stand for eight. Here are the addition and multiplication tables for the eight-scale:

EIGHT-SCALE ADDITION TABLE

	0	1	2	3	4	5	6	7
0	0	1	2	3	4	5	6	7
1	1	2	3	4	5	6	7	10
2	2	3	4	5	6	7	10	11
3	3	4	5	6	7	10	11	12
4	4	5	6	7	10	11	12	13
5	5	6	7	10	11	12	13	14
6	6	7	10	11	12	13	14	15
7	7	10	11	12	13	14	15	16

EIGHT-SCALE MULTIPLICATION TABLE

	0	1	2	3	4	5	6	7
0	0	0	0	0	0	0	0	0
1	0	1	2	3	4	5	6	7
2	0	2	4	6	10	12	14	16
3	0	3	6	11	14	17	22	25
4	0	4	10	14	20	24	30	34
5	0	5	12	17	24	31	36	43
6	0	6	14	22	30	36	44	52
7	0	7	16	25	34	43	52	61

To interpret these written numbers correctly, remember that the digit in the second column from the right tells you how many eights to use. The number 52 means 5 eights plus 2, or forty-two. That's why $7 \times 6 = 52$ in the eight-scale.

In the space below, one addition example is done in two ways. On the left, the numbers are added in the ten-scale. On the right, the same numbers are written the way they

33

look in the eight-scale, and they are added according to the rules of the eight-scale. In the ten-scale, 5 plus 7 is 12, so we put down the 2 and carry the 1. Then 1 plus 4 plus 3 gives 8, and the answer is 82. In the eight-scale, forty-five is written as 55, because that means 5 eights plus 5. Thirty-seven is written as 45, because that means 4 eights plus five. For the addition, we use the eight-scale addition table. There we see that 5 plus 5 is 12, so we put down the 2 and carry the 1. Then 1 plus 5 plus 4 is 12, so again we put down the 2 and carry the 1. Then the answer is 122. In the eight-scale this means sixty-four plus two eights plus 2, or eighty-two, the same answer we got in the ten-scale addition.

TEN-SCALE ADDITION:	EIGHT-SCALE ADDITION
45	55
+ 37	+ 45
82	122

The numbers below are written in the eight-scale. Add them by the rules of the eight-scale:

32	65	113	235	77
+ 14	+ 24	+ 51	+ 154	+ 77

Check your answers by rewriting all the numbers in the ten-scale. (Answer No. 3)

On the next page, one multiplication example is done in two ways. On the left, the numbers are multiplied in the ten-scale. On the right, the same numbers are written the way they look in the eight-scale, and they are multiplied according to the rules of the eight-scale. The answers agree, because 1,766 in the eight-scale means five hundred

34

twelve plus 7 sixty-fours plus 6 eights plus 6. This adds up to 1,014 in the ten-scale.

Ten-Scale Multiplication	Eight-Scale Multiplication
39	47
× 26	× 32
234	116
78	165
1014	1766

The numbers below are written in the eight-scale. Multiply them by the rules of the eight-scale

$$\begin{array}{ccc} 17 & 106 & 13 \\ \times 42 & \times 45 & \times 31 \end{array}$$

Check your answers by rewriting all the numbers in the ten-scale. (Answer No. 4)

Changing to the Eight-Scale

To change a number from the ten-scale to the eight-scale, we have to break it up into groups of eight, eight times eight, eight times eight times eight, and so on. To do this, first divide the number by 8. Write the quotient on the next line, and write the remainder on the side. Then divide the quotient by 8, put the new quotient on the next line, and the remainder on the side. We keep this up until we get a quotient equal to zero. The remainders we get are the digits we use to write the number in the eight-scale. The order in which we get them is the order of the digits from right to left. The example below shows how the work is arranged:

35

$$8 \overline{)651}$$ Remainders

$$8 \overline{)81} \ldots \ldots \ldots \ldots \ldots \ldots 3$$

$$8 \overline{)10} \ldots \ldots \ldots \ldots \ldots \ldots 1$$

$$8 \overline{)1} \ldots \ldots \ldots \ldots \ldots \ldots 2$$

$$0 \ldots \ldots \ldots \ldots \ldots \ldots 1$$

So the ten-scale number 651 is written as 1,213 in the eight-scale. Follow the same scheme to find out how each of these ten-scale numbers is written in the eight-scale:

53   154   1067   (Answer No. 5)

If We Had Twelve Fingers

Some people are born with six fingers on a hand, so they have twelve fingers altogether. If we all had twelve fingers, it would be natural to count things out in groups of twelve instead of groups of ten. As a matter of fact, we do it even now, when we count things by the dozen, or measure lengths by the foot, where 12 inches equals 1 foot. If we used groups of twelve all the time, it would be convenient to write our numbers in a twelve-scale instead of the ten-scale we use today.

To write numbers in a twelve-scale we need a separate digit for every number up to eleven. For the first ten digits we can use the digits of the ten-scale: 0, 1, 2, 3, 4, 5, 6, 7, 8, and 9. But for the next two numbers we have to invent new digits. Let us use T to stand for ten, and E to stand for eleven. Then, with these twelve digits, we can write every other number, by using more than one column. A 1 in the second column from the right would mean twelve. A 1 in the third column would mean twelve times twelve, or one hundred forty-four. A 1 in the fourth column would mean twelve times twelve times twelve, or one thousand seven hundred twenty-eight. In the twelve-scale,

10 means 1 twelve plus 0, or twelve. The number 11 means 1 twelve plus 1, or thirteen. The number 1T means 1 twelve plus ten, or twenty-two. The number 1E means 1 twelve plus eleven, or twenty-three. The number 31T means 3 times one hundred forty-four plus 1 twelve plus ten, or 454 in the ten-scale.

The numbers below are written in the twelve-scale. How would the same numbers be written in the ten-scale?

1T3   524   19   TET   20E   (Answer No. 6)

Changing to the Twelve-Scale

To change a number from the ten-scale to the twelve-scale, divide the number by twelve, write the quotient on the next line, and write the remainder on the side. Then divide the quotient by twelve, put the new quotient on the next line, and the remainder on the side. Keep this up until you get a quotient equal to zero. If you get a remainder of ten or eleven, remember to use the symbols T or E. The remainders will be the digits of the number written in the twelve-scale. The order in which the remainders appear is the order of the digits from right to left. The example below shows how the work is arranged:

$$12)\overline{3875} \qquad \text{Remainders}$$
$$12)\overline{322}\dots\dots\dots\dots E$$
$$12)\overline{26}\dots\dots\dots\dots T$$
$$12)\overline{2}\dots\dots\dots\dots 2$$
$$0\dots\dots\dots\dots 2$$

So the ten-scale number 3,875 is written as 22TE in the twelve-scale. Follow the same scheme to find out how each of these ten-scale numbers is written in the twelve-scale:

1769   310   1596   (Answer No. 7)

Twelve-Scale Arithmetic

To do arithmetic examples in the twelve-scale you have to use the twelve-scale addition and multiplication tables. Here they are:

TWELVE-SCALE ADDITION TABLE

	0	1	2	3	4	5	6	7	8	9	T	E
0	0	1	2	3	4	5	6	7	8	9	T	E
1	1	2	3	4	5	6	7	8	9	T	E	10
2	2	3	4	5	6	7	8	9	T	E	10	11
3	3	4	5	6	7	8	9	T	E	10	11	12
4	4	5	6	7	8	9	T	E	10	11	12	13
5	5	6	7	8	9	T	E	10	11	12	13	14
6	6	7	8	9	T	E	10	11	12	13	14	15
7	7	8	9	T	E	10	11	12	13	14	15	16
8	8	9	T	E	10	11	12	13	14	15	16	17
9	9	T	E	10	11	12	13	14	15	16	17	18
T	T	E	10	11	12	13	14	15	16	17	18	19
E	E	10	11	12	13	14	15	16	17	18	19	1T

TWELVE-SCALE MULTIPLICATION TABLE

	0	1	2	3	4	5	6	7	8	9	T	E
0	0	0	0	0	0	0	0	0	0	0	0	0
1	0	1	2	3	4	5	6	7	8	9	T	E
2	0	2	4	6	8	T	10	12	14	16	18	1T
3	0	3	6	9	10	13	16	19	20	23	26	29
4	0	4	8	10	14	18	20	24	28	30	34	38
5	0	5	T	13	18	21	26	2E	34	39	42	47
6	0	6	10	16	20	26	30	36	40	46	50	56
7	0	7	12	19	24	2E	36	41	48	53	5T	65
8	0	8	14	20	28	34	40	48	54	60	68	74
9	0	9	16	23	30	39	46	53	60	69	76	83
T	0	T	18	26	34	42	50	5T	68	76	84	92
E	0	E	1T	29	38	47	56	65	74	83	92	T1

The numbers below are written in the twelve-scale. Add them by the rules of the twelve-scale:

$$
\begin{array}{ccccc}
58 & 27 & \text{T1T} & 43 & 68 \\
+\,14 & +\,1\text{E} & +\,1\text{ET} & +\,58 & +\,19
\end{array}
$$

Check your answers by rewriting all the numbers in the ten-scale. (Answer No. 8)

The numbers below are written in the twelve-scale. Multiply them by the rules of the twelve-scale:

$$
\begin{array}{ccc}
123 & 87 & 34 \\
\times\ \text{TE} & \times\,45 & \times\,80
\end{array}
$$

Check your answers by rewriting all the numbers in the ten-scale. (Answer No. 9)

The Schoolboy's Dream

A boy who had trouble remembering his multiplication tables once had a wonderful dream. He dreamed that his arithmetic teacher told him he did not have to study addition or multiplication tables for any numbers higher than 1. He learned the answers for $0 + 0$, $0 + 1$, $1 + 0$, and $1 + 1$. Then he learned the answers for 0×0, 0×1, 1×0, and 1×1. With these eight answers he was able to do any example in addition or multiplication. The strangest part about this dream is that it could be true! We can make it true by writing our numbers in a two-scale instead of a ten-scale.

To write numbers in the scale based on groups of two, we need only two digits, the figures 0 and 1. We don't need a separate digit for the number two, because two makes a full group, and we show a group of two by putting a 1 in the second column from the right. Then 10 means 1 group of two plus 0, or *two*. The written number 11 would mean

39

1 group of two plus 1, or *three*. A 1 in the third column from the right would mean two times two, or *four*. A 1 in the fourth column would mean *eight,* in the fifth column it would mean *sixteen,* and so on.

The numbers below are written in the two-scale. How would the same numbers be written in the ten-scale?

100   101   110   1010   1111   (Answer No. 10)

Changing to the Two-Scale

To change a number from the ten-scale to the two-scale, divide the number by two, write the quotient on the next line, and write the remainder on the side. Then divide the quotient by two, put the new quotient on the next line, and the remainder on the side. Keep this up until you get a quotient equal to zero. The remainders will be the digits of the number written in the two-scale. The order in which the remainders appear is the order of the digits from right to left. The example below shows how the work is arranged:

$$2)\overline{21} \qquad\qquad \text{Remainders}$$
$$2)\overline{10} \ldots\ldots\ldots\ldots\ldots 1$$
$$2)\overline{5} \ldots\ldots\ldots\ldots\ldots 0$$
$$2)\overline{2} \ldots\ldots\ldots\ldots\ldots 1$$
$$2)\overline{1} \ldots\ldots\ldots\ldots\ldots 0$$
$$0 \ldots\ldots\ldots\ldots\ldots 1$$

So the ten-scale number 21 is written as 10,101 in the two-scale. To check this result remember that the first digit from the right tells you how many ones to take; the second digit tells you how many twos to take; the third digit tells you how many fours to take; the fourth digit tells you how many eights to take; the fifth digit tells you how many sixteens to take. Then 10,101 means sixteen plus four plus one, or 21 in the ten-scale.

Follow the same scheme of repeated division by two to find out how each of these ten-scale numbers is written in the two-scale:

35   7   83   10   5   (Answer No. 11)

The Dream Comes True

The schoolboy's dream comes true in the addition and multiplication tables of the two-scale. Here they are:

	TWO-SCALE ADDITION TABLE			TWO-SCALE MULTIPLICATION TABLE	
	0	1		0	1
0	0	1	0	0	0
1	1	10	1	0	1

One way of getting acquainted with numbers written in the two-scale is to start with the number 1, and then, using the addition table, add a series of ones, one at a time. In this way, you get the numbers one, two, three, four, five, and so on, in order:

$$
\begin{array}{ccccccc}
1 & 1 & 10 & 11 & 100 & 101 & 110 & 111 \\
+1 & +1 & +1 & +1 & +1 & +1 & +1 \\
\hline
10 & 11 & 100 & 101 & 110 & 111 & 1000
\end{array}
$$

Add more ones to continue the series until you reach the number sixteen. (Answer No. 12)

The numbers below are written in the two-scale. Add them by the rules of two-scale addition:

$$
\begin{array}{ccccc}
101 & 11 & 11 & 10101 & 111 \\
+110 & +10 & +11 & +1010 & +11
\end{array}
$$

41

Check your answers by rewriting all the numbers in the ten-scale. (Answer No. 13)

The numbers below are written in the two-scale. Multiply them by the rules of the two-scale:

$$
\begin{array}{ccc}
101 & 111 & 10101 \\
\times\ 10 & \times\ 11 & \times\ 101
\end{array}
$$

Check your answers by rewriting all the numbers in the ten-scale. (Answer No. 14)

Flip-Flop Circuits

The two-scale, or binary scale, as it is usually called, is not merely the lazy schoolboy's dream come true. It has an important use in modern electronic calculators. Your electric light switch helps to explain the reason why. There are two positions of the switch. One turns the electric current on. The other turns it off. These two positions can be represented by the symbols 1 and 0: 1 for on, and 0 for off. So the positions of the switch can be read as the digits 0, or 1. Then a series of switches can be read as a number in the binary scale. Suppose, for example, there are three switches in a line, each controlling a separate neon lamp. Then the different possible positions of the switches give various combinations of lit and unlit lamps, and these can be used to represent the numbers from zero to seven in this way:

OFF OFF OFF	means	000, or the number zero;
OFF OFF ON	means	001, or the number one;
OFF ON OFF	means	010, or the number two;
OFF ON ON	means	011, or the number three;
ON OFF OFF	means	100, or the number four;
ON OFF ON	means	101, or the number five;
ON ON OFF	means	110, or the number six;
ON ON ON	means	111, or the number seven.

42

In binary-scale addition, when you add 1 and 1, you get 10, which means put down a 0, and carry 1 to the next column to the left. In electronic calculators, the addition is done in this way with the help of a special electronic circuit that engineers call a *flip-flop circuit*. There is a separate flip-flop circuit controlling each switch and its neon lamp, and these circuits are connected in order. Numbers are recorded by feeding electrical pulses into the first circuit. When this circuit receives no pulses, the switch it controls is OFF. When it receives one pulse, it turns the switch on. When it receives a second pulse, it turns the switch off again, and passes a pulse on to the next circuit on the left. This is like putting down a zero and carrying a 1 to the next column. In the same way, each circuit, after receiving two pulses, turns off the switch that it controls, and passes on a pulse to the next circuit on the left. To add the numbers three and four, we would first feed three pulses, and then four more, into the first flip-flop circuit. To trace the action of the calculator, look again at the chart above, showing positions of the first three switches, controlled by the first three flip-flop circuits. The first line of the chart shows the positions of the switches before any pulses are fed into the machine. The second line shows the positions after the first pulse; the next line shows the positions after the second pulse, and so on. After the third pulse, the switches are in the positions OFF ON ON, showing the binary number 011, or three. After the next four pulses, the switches are in the positions ON ON ON, showing the binary number 111, or seven.

A Numbers Wardrobe

There are many different kinds of clothing that a girl can wear. The clothing that she will choose from her wardrobe at any time depends on what she is going to do. She may put on a skirt and blouse when she goes to school, a dress when she goes to a party, dungarees when she works in the garden, and a bathing suit when she goes swimming. There is a form of dress that is best for every occasion.

A number, too, has many dresses that it can wear. These dresses are the ways in which we write the number in different scales. The number fifteen, for example, is written as 15 in the ten-scale, 13 in the twelve-scale, 17 in the eight-scale, and 1,111 in the binary scale. The dresses are different, but the number is the same. We choose a dress for a number the way we choose clothing for ourselves. We choose the dress that is best suited to what we are going to do. For ordinary arithmetic we use the ten-scale. But if we plan to use an electronic calculator, we dress our numbers up in the two-scale. When we play the games and do the tricks described later in this book, we shall use the scale that will make our work easiest. Most of the time we shall use the ten-scale, but there are places where we shall use the two-scale, or binary scale, instead.

CHAPTER III

The Personalities of Numbers

The Shapes of Numbers

THE multiples of nine, written in the ten-scale, are 9, 18, 27, 36, 45, and so on. If you add the digits in any one of these numbers, and then add the digits of the sum, repeating the process until you have only one digit, the result is always 9. For example, adding the digits of 27, we get $2 + 7 = 9$. Adding the digits of 729, we get $7 + 2 + 9 = 18$, but $1 + 8 = 9$. But if twenty-seven is written in the eight-scale instead of the ten-scale, then we write it as 33 instead of 27. Then the sum of its digits is 6. If seven hundred twenty-nine is written in the eight-scale, then we write it as 1,331 instead of 729. Then the sum of its digits is 10 by the addition rules of the eight-scale, and $1 + 0 = 1$. So the rule, "adding the digits of a multiple of nine gives 9 as a final result," is true *only when the numbers are written in the ten-scale.* The fact which the rule describes is a fact about the way the number is written, rather than a fact about the number itself. All of the curious facts we saw in Chapter I are like this one. They depend on the scale in which the numbers are written. They are features of the dresses the numbers wear.

But there are some features of numbers that do not depend on the scale in which the numbers are written. They show the real personalities of the numbers, and they are true no matter what dresses the numbers wear when we write them down. We can find features like these by not

45

dressing the numbers in any scale at all. We can go back to the old system of representing a number by a collection of pebbles, or by a collection of checkers. Then we shall find clues to the personalities of numbers in the shapes of the patterns in which the pebbles or checkers can be arranged.

Triangle Numbers

Ten checkers can be arranged to form a triangle, as shown in the drawing below. The triangle is made up of a

```
    o

   o  o

  o  o  o

 o  o  o  o
```

series of lines of checkers that are placed one above the other. The longest line is at the bottom, and each of the other lines has one checker less than the line that is just below it. Because ten checkers can be arranged in a pattern like this, the number *ten* is called a *triangle number*. If we remove the bottom line of four checkers, what is left is another triangle made up of six checkers, so the number *six* is also a triangle number. If we now remove the line of three checkers, what is left is the triangle number *three*. If we remove the line of two checkers, we find that the smallest triangle number is the number *one*.

Now if we reverse the process, we can get all the triangle numbers in the order of their size. First put down one checker. Then, under it, put down two checkers in a line. Under the line of two checkers, put a line of three checkers; under the line of three checkers, put a line of

46

four checkers; under the line of four checkers, put a line of five checkers; and so on. Put into each new line one more checker than the line above it has. The number of checkers in the longest line of a triangle is equal to the number of lines in the triangle. Each triangle number is the sum of all the whole numbers from 1 up to the number of lines in the triangle. The first ten triangle numbers are:

$$1 = 1$$
$$1 + 2 = 3$$
$$1 + 2 + 3 = 6$$
$$1 + 2 + 3 + 4 = 10$$
$$1 + 2 + 3 + 4 + 5 = 15$$
$$1 + 2 + 3 + 4 + 5 + 6 = 21$$
$$1 + 2 + 3 + 4 + 5 + 6 + 7 = 28$$
$$1 + 2 + 3 + 4 + 5 + 6 + 7 + 8 = 36$$
$$1 + 2 + 3 + 4 + 5 + 6 + 7 + 8 + 9 = 45$$
$$1 + 2 + 3 + 4 + 5 + 6 + 7 + 8 + 9 + 10 = 55$$

For convenience in talking about a triangle number we shall sometimes use a special way of referring to it: We shall write the letter T followed by a number in parentheses, telling us what place the triangle number occupies when all the triangle numbers are arranged in order of size. Then $T(4)$ means the fourth triangle number, or 10. What numbers are meant by $T(11)$ and $T(12)$? (Answer No. 15)

Suppose we wanted to find out what the twenty-fifth triangle number, $T(25)$, is equal to. One way of finding out would be to start with the first triangle number, 1. Add 2 to get the second; add 3 to get the third; add 4 to get the fourth, and so on. If we do it this way, to find the twenty-fifth triangle number we would have to find the twenty-four smaller ones first. That makes it a rather long and, slow process. Fortunately, we can use a short-cut.

47

To find the short-cut, let us first use another way to find out what number is meant by T(4). Take two sets of checkers, each arranged in a triangle of four rows. One set has the longest line at the bottom. The other set is upside down, so it has the longest line at the top. Now let us put the two triangles side by side, as shown in the drawing.

○ ● ● ● ●

○ ○ ● ● ●

○ ○ ○ ● ●

○ ○ ○ ○ ●

The result is a rectangle. The number of lines in the rectangle is the same as the number of lines each triangle has. The number of checkers in each line of the rectangle is one more than that number. So if we multiply the number of lines in the triangle by the next higher number, we find the number of checkers in the rectangle. But the rectangle has twice as many checkers as each triangle has alone. So if we divide the product by 2, we get the number of checkers in each triangle. In this case we are finding T(4). The triangle for it has 4 lines. Multiply 4×5, and divide by 2, and we find that T(4) = 10. We can find any other triangle number in the same way. Take the number that shows the place of the triangle number in order of size, multiply by the next higher number, and then divide by 2. By this short-cut we find that T(25) equals 25×26 divided by 2. So T(25) = 325.

Use the short-cut to find T(15), T(20), and T(100). (Answer No. 16)

Square Numbers

Another special shape that can be formed from lines of

48

```
O      O O      O O O      O O O O
       O O      O O O      O O O O
                O O O      O O O O
                           O O O O
```

checkers is a square. To form a square, put down any number of lines, one under the other, with as many checkers in each line as there are lines. The smallest square has one line with one checker in the line. The next square has two lines with two checkers in each line. The third square has three lines with three checkers in each line, and so on. The number of checkers needed to make a square is called a *square number*. Because of the way the square is formed we see that the first square number is 1×1, or 1; the second square number is 2×2, or 4; the third square number is 3×3, or 9, and so on. To get a square number, multiply any whole number by itself. It has become a custom to show this multiplication by a special kind of shorthand in which the multiplier is written down, and a small 2 is written after it in the upper right-hand corner to show that the multiplier is used twice. So, to show the fourth square number, we write 4^2. We read it as "four-square," and it means 4×4, or 16. To show the fifth square number, we write 5^2. We read it as "five-square," and it means 5×5, or 25. What square numbers are represented by the symbols 6^2, 7^2, 10^2, 13^2? (Answer No. 17)

The square numbers are relatives of the odd numbers, 1, 3, 5, 7, 9, 11, and so on. If we take any number of these odd numbers in order, starting with 1, and add them up, the sum is always a square number:

$$1 = 1 = 1^2$$
$$1 + 3 = 4 = 2^2$$
$$1 + 3 + 5 = 9 = 3^2$$
$$1 + 3 + 5 + 7 = 16 = 4^2$$
$$1 + 3 + 5 + 7 + 9 = 25 = 5^2$$

49

The reason for this interesting connection is shown in the drawing below. We can get the square numbers in order by starting with a square that contains only one checker,

and then gradually making the square longer and wider by adding more checkers. The checkers added at each step are shown between the L-shaped lines. The first group added contains three checkers; the next group contains five checkers, and so on.

The square numbers are also relatives of the triangle numbers. If you add any triangle number to the next higher triangle number, the result is always a square number:

$$T(1) + T(2) = 1 + 3 = 4 = 2^2$$
$$T(2) + T(3) = 3 + 6 = 9 = 3^2$$
$$T(3) + T(4) = 6 + 10 = 16 = 4^2$$
$$T(4) + T(5) = 10 + 15 = 25 = 5^2$$

The reason for this connection is shown in the drawing below. A line divides each square into two triangles, showing that each square number is the sum of two triangle numbers.

50

The square numbers are related to the triangle numbers in another way, too. If you take eight times any triangle number and add 1, the result is always a square number:

$$T(1) = 1. \quad 8 \times 1 + 1 = 9 = 3^2$$
$$T(2) = 3. \quad 8 \times 3 + 1 = 25 = 5^2$$
$$T(3) = 6. \quad 8 \times 6 + 1 = 49 = 7^2$$
$$T(4) = 10. \quad 8 \times 10 + 1 = 81 = 9^2$$
$$T(5) = 15. \quad 8 \times 15 + 1 = 121 = 11^2$$

Notice, too, how the odd numbers, 3, 5, 7, 9, 11, and so on, come into the picture again.

Mathematicians have been fascinated by the triangle numbers and square numbers for many centuries. They tried to find as many connections as they could between ordinary numbers and these numbers that have special shapes. One of the interesting discoveries they made is that every whole number is the sum of three triangle numbers or less. They also found that every whole number is the sum of four square numbers or less. For example, $48 = T(9) + T(2)$, and $48 = 4^2 + 4^2 + 4^2$. Find two triangle numbers that add up to 150. Find three square numbers that add up to 150. (Answer No. 18)

Cubic Numbers

If we use a baby's blocks instead of checkers, we can arrange them side by side to form square layers one block high, and then, by piling up equal layers, we can make cubes. We need one block to make the smallest cube. To make the second cube, first make a line of two blocks. Two of these lines make a square layer. Two of these layers make the cube. So the number of blocks needed is $2 \times 2 \times 2$, or 8. To make the third cube, first make a line of three blocks. Three of these lines make a square layer. Three of these layers make the cube. So the number of blocks needed is $3 \times 3 \times 3$, or 27. To make the fourth cube, $4 \times 4 \times 4$, or 64 blocks are needed. The number of blocks needed to make a cube is called a *cubic number*. To get a

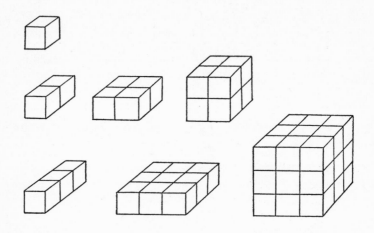

cubic number, multiply any whole number by itself, and then again by itself, so that the same number is used as a multiplier three times. Cubic numbers are shown by the same kind of shorthand we used to write down square numbers. The multiplier is written down, and a small 3 is written after it in the upper right-hand corner to show that the multiplier is used three times. To show the second cubic number, for example, we write 2^3. We read it as "two-cube," and it means $2 \times 2 \times 2$, or 8. To show the fifth cubic number we write 5^3. We read it as "five-cube," and it means $5 \times 5 \times 5$, or 125. What cubic numbers are represented by the symbols 6^3, 7^3, 10^3? (Answer No. 19)

The cubic numbers, like the square numbers from which we build them, are also related to the odd numbers. If the odd numbers are listed in a line, the first one gives the first cubic number, the next two add up to the second cubic number, the next three after them add up to the third cubic number, and so on:

52

$$\begin{array}{cccc}
1 & 3+5 & 7+9+11 & 13+15+17+19 \\
1 & 8 & 27 & 64
\end{array}$$

$$21+23+25+27+29$$
$$125$$

The cubic numbers are also related to the triangle numbers in a rather peculiar way. If we add all the cubic numbers in order, starting with 1, the sums are always the squares of triangle numbers:

$1^3 = 1 = 1^2$, and $1 = T(1)$.
$1^3 + 2^3 = 9 = 3^2$, and $3 = T(2)$.
$1^3 + 2^3 + 3^3 = 36 = 6^2$, and $6 = T(3)$.
$1^3 + 2^3 + 3^3 + 4^3 = 100 = 10^2$, and $10 = T(4)$.
$1^3 + 2^3 + 3^3 + 4^3 + 5^3 = 225 = 15^2$, and $15 = T(5)$.

In the year 1772 a British mathematician named Edward Waring announced that every number was the sum of nine cubic numbers or less, but he did not prove his statement. The statement turned out to be true, but it took other mathematicians 139 years to prove it.

Perfect Numbers

The numbers less than 6 that are divisors of 6 are 1, 2, and 3. But $1 + 2 + 3 = 6$, the number whose divisors we added. This is an unusual personality trait of a number. Most numbers do not have it. For example, the numbers less than 12 that are divisors of 12 are 1, 2, 3, 4, and 6. But $1 + 2 + 3 + 4 + 6$ is not equal to 12. When the mathematicians of ancient Greece found a few rare numbers that did have this trait, they were so impressed with them that they called them *perfect numbers*. A perfect number is a number that is equal to the sum of all of its divisors that are less than itself. The next three perfect numbers after 6 are 28, 496, and 8,128. It took about 1400 years after the days of ancient Greece before the fifth perfect number was discovered. It turned out to be 33,550,336. The sixth perfect number is 8,589,869,056. Up to the present time only seventeen perfect numbers have been discovered. The seventeenth perfect number is so big it has 1,373 digits when it is written in the ordinary ten-scale. If it were written out on this page, it would fill the whole page.

Prove that 28 and 496 and 8,128 are perfect numbers. (Answer No. 20)

CHAPTER IV

Puzzles With Numbers

Dividing the Milk

"GOOD morning, Mrs. Jones," said Mrs. Smith. "May I borrow your five-quart pail today? I am going to the store to buy four quarts of milk, and my pail isn't big enough. It holds only three quarts."

"I was just about to go to the store myself, to buy four quarts too," said Mrs. Jones. "Suppose you take my eight-quart pail. Have it filled, and we'll divide the milk when you get back."

Mrs. Smith returned from the store with the eight-quart pail full of milk. Then, with the help of the five-quart pail and the three-quart pail, Mrs. Jones divided the milk into two equal parts. How did she do it? (Answer No. 21)

The Farmer's Bequest

The lawyer solemnly broke the seal on the will of the late farmer Brown. Seated at the table with him were the farmer's three sons, Tom, Dick, and Harry, and their neighbor, farmer Green. The lawyer opened the folded paper, and began to read: "I bequeath my seventeen cows to my three sons, to be divided as follows: one half of the cows to my eldest, Tom; one third of the cows to Dick; and one ninth of the cows to my youngest, Harry."

The lawyer put down the will, took out a pencil, and did some rapid figuring on a pad. Then he said, "That means that Tom gets 8½ cows, Dick gets 5⅔ cows, and

Harry gets $1\frac{5}{9}$ cows." He smiled, very pleased with himself for being so learned and clever.

"You may be very good in arithmetic," Tom said somewhat sourly, "but it is obvious you don't know anything about farming. Half of a cow is half of a dead cow, and dead cows don't give any milk."

"His arithmetic is no good either," said Harry. "If you add $8\frac{1}{2}$, $5\frac{2}{3}$, and $1\frac{5}{9}$, the sum is only $16\frac{1}{18}$." The three sons glared suspiciously at the lawyer, wondering if he was trying to cheat them out of $\frac{17}{18}$ of a cow. The lawyer looked helplessly toward farmer Green, and shrugged his shoulders.

Farmer Green stroked his beard calmly, and said, "Keep your tempers, boys. I know how you can divide the cows as your father wished, without killing any cows, and with no pieces of cows left over. Just wait here while I go to my barn." When he returned from his barn, he showed them how the will could be carried out, to the sons' satisfaction and the lawyer's great relief. How was it done? (Answer No. 22)

The Counterfeit Coin

The coin dealer went to the case for the eight rare coins he was taking with him. If he hurried, he could make the three o'clock plane. His face fell when he opened the case. "Omigosh!" he exclaimed. "Somebody put the counterfeit coin into the tray with the eight genuine coins. The counterfeit is lighter than the others, but I don't have time to weigh them one by one." "You don't have to," his assistant said. "We can weigh the coins against each other on this balance scale, and pick out the counterfeit in only two weighings." The assistant was right. In two weighings he quickly found the counterfeit coin. The dealer rushed to the airport with the others, and boarded the plane five seconds before it took off. How did his assistant pick out the counterfeit coin? (Answer No. 23)

In the Marketplace

The inquisitive tourist looked at the five different weights standing in a line beside the balance scale on Abu's counter in the marketplace. "Are those five weights enough," he asked, "to measure out any weight your customers ask for?"

"By putting one or more of these weights on one pan," Abu replied, "I can weigh out on the other pan any whole number of pounds from 1 to 31."

His neighbor, Mustapha, overhearing them, broke into the conversation. "I do better than that," he said. "I have only four weights. But, by putting weights on both pans of my scale, I can weigh out any whole number of pounds from 1 to 40."

What are the five weights that Abu uses? What are the four weights that Mustapha uses? (Answer No. 24)

Uphill and Downhill

An automobile went up a hill at a speed of 10 miles per hour, and returned downhill at a speed of 20 miles per hour. What was the average speed for the round trip? (Answer No. 25)

Returning from Chicago

An automobile went from New York to Chicago at an average speed of 30 miles per hour. How fast would it have to come back to make the average speed for the round trip 60 miles per hour? (Answer No. 26)

The Hands of a Clock

The hands of a clock are together at 12 noon. At what time in the afternoon will they next be together again? (Answer No. 27)

The Train and the Tunnel

A freight train one mile long goes through a tunnel that is one mile long. If the train is traveling at a speed of 15 miles per hour, how long does it take to pass through the tunnel? (Answer No. 28)

Passing Trains

Every hour, on the hour, a train leaves New York for Philadelphia, while another train leaves Philadelphia for New York. The trip between the two cities takes exactly two hours. When a train goes from New York to Philadelphia, how many of the trains going in the opposite direction will it meet? (Answer No. 29)

A Sad Story

Two bicycles start traveling toward each other at the same time from places that are 250 miles apart. One of them travels at a speed of 10 miles per hour, while the other one goes 15 miles per hour. At the moment that they start, a fly named Agamemnon leaves the front wheel of the slower bicycle, and flying at a speed of 20 miles per hour, heads toward the other bicycle. As soon as he touches its front wheel, he turns right around and flies back. As the bicycles approach each other, he continues flying back and forth, touching each front wheel in turn, until, alas, poor Agamemnon is crushed between the two front wheels. How many trips back and forth does Agamemnon make before his sad fate overtakes him? How far does he travel altogether? (Answer No. 30)

100 Items, 100 Cents

A girl bought some pencils, erasers, and paper clips at the stationery store. The pencils cost 10¢ each, the erasers cost 5¢ each, and the clips cost 2 for 1¢. If she bought 100 things altogether at a total cost of $1, how many pencils, how many erasers, and how many clips did she buy? (Answer No. 31)

The Extra Square

On graph paper that is cross-ruled into squares, draw a large square that is 8 squares long and 8 squares high. The area of the large square is 8 × 8, or 64 small squares. Divide the large square into four pieces, as shown by the dark lines in the drawing below. These four pieces can be rearranged to form a rectangle 13 squares long and 5

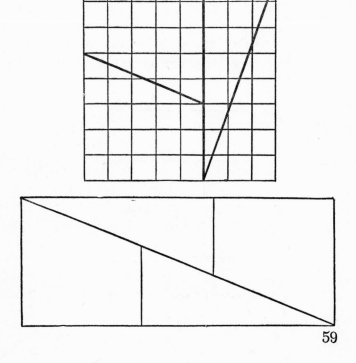

squares high. Then the area is 13×5, or 65 small squares. Where did the extra square come from? (Answer No. 32)

The Missing Penny

Every day Mrs. Jones went to the marketplace with 30 apples which she sold at 2 for 1 cent. If she sold them all, she brought home 15 cents. Her friend and neighbor, Mrs. Smith, also went to the marketplace each day with 30 apples that she sold at 3 for 1 cent. If she sold them all, she brought home 10 cents. One day Mrs. Smith was sick, so Mrs. Jones offered to sell her apples along with her own. She sold the mixed apples at 5 for 2 cents. When she settled accounts with Mrs. Smith at the end of the day, she was embarrassed to find that she had only 24 cents instead of the 25 cents she expected. How had she lost the missing penny? (Answer No. 33)

Magic Squares

Make a square, divided like the one shown below, into 3×3 or 9 boxes. Put into each box one of the numbers from 1 to 9, using each number once and only once. Try

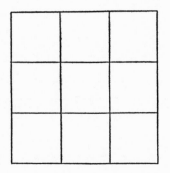

1,2,3,4,5,6,7,8,9

to get an arrangement in which the numbers in each horizontal row, each vertical column, and each diagonal add up to the same amount. Such an arrangement is called a *magic square.*

First let us figure out how much each row should add up to. The sum of all the numbers from 1 to 9 is the ninth triangle number $T(9)$, or 45. Since there are three rows, each row must add up to 45 divided by 3, or 15. Make the magic square now, and then compare your answer with the one in the answer section. (Answer No. 34)

After you have made a magic square with the numbers from 1 to 9, try to make one with the numbers from 1 to 25. Arrange them in a 5×5 square, so that each row, each column, and each diagonal add up to 65. (Answer No. 35)

CHAPTER V

Puzzles Without Numbers

Crossing the River

A FARMER was on his way to town with a lamb and a cabbage he was taking to market, and a wolf he was taking to the zoo. To get them across a river that lay between his farm and the town, he had to ferry them across in a rowboat. But the boat was so small, it could carry only one of them at a time besides himself. He could not leave the wolf alone with the lamb, because the wolf would eat the lamb. He could not leave the lamb alone with the cabbage, because then the lamb would eat the cabbage. How did he manage to get all three of them, safe and uneaten, over to the other side? (Answer No. 36)

The Census

The census taker, counting the inhabitants of a backwoods parish, was questioning the bearded owner of a tumbledown shack. He pointed to another bearded gent who lay fast asleep, propped up against a tree. "Who is he?" he asked. The man replied, "Brothers and sisters have I none, but that man's father is my father's son." Who was the sleeping man? (Answer No. 37)

The Race to Mecca

Old Mohammed was a strange man in death as in life. His last will and testament decreed that his two sons should run a race to Mecca, on camels. The whole estate, the old man had written, will go to the one whose camel gets to Mecca *last*. The sons, always respectful and obedient, were trying hard to carry out the terms of his will, but were having great difficulty doing so. Each of them was naturally anxious to win the coveted prize. So each of them was in no hurry to get to Mecca. They dawdled, dallied, delayed, and backtracked, each hoping the other would forget himself and enter Mecca first. The race had been going on for two weeks, when they dismounted, tired, hungry, and depressed, and wept on each other's shoulders. Just then a wise man happened to pass by, and he stopped to ask the cause of their grief. They explained their sad case as he listened attentively. When they finished their tale, he said, "Your troubles are not as bad as you think," and he told them how they could carry out their father's will without delay. As soon as the wise man finished speaking, the brothers jumped on the camels and rushed off to Mecca at top speed. What did the wise man tell them? (Answer No. 38)

The Bad Omen

The night watchman timidly shuffled across the carpet that covered the floor of the office. He had never spoken to the president of the firm before. He had never been in an office that was so large, nor had he ever walked on a carpet that was so soft. He passed his cap from hand to hand as the president smiled benignly and said, "Well, my good man, what can I do for you today?"

"Excuse me, sir," he said, "for interrupting you. I know you are busy. But this is very important. I know you are planning to fly to Chicago this afternoon for the week-end convention. Please don't fly. Take the train instead."

The president was visibly surprised. He had tried to figure out why the night watchman had asked to see him. He had been prepared to hear him ask for a raise, or for a day off. But this request was entirely unexpected, and somewhat disturbing. The temperature of his smile dropped a few degrees as he said, "That's a rather strange thing to ask. Why shouldn't I fly?"

"Well, you see, sir. Last night I had a dream that the plane to Chicago crashed, and all aboard were killed. It's a bad omen. Please don't tempt the fates. Take the train."

The president's smile warmed up again as he walked the night watchman to the door. "Thanks for telling me," he said, and shook his hand.

In spite of the warning, the president flew to Chicago. The plane arrived safely. The convention was interesting, but otherwise uneventful. On Monday, he flew back to New York. As soon as he stepped back into his office he ordered that the night watchman be fired. Why did he fire him? (Answer No. 39)

Smoke Screen

If an electric train heads north at a speed of 80 miles per hour, and the wind blows from the east at a speed of 20 miles per hour, in what direction will the smoke of the train trail off? (Answer No. 40)

Squaring the Cross

Cut out a piece of cardboard in the shape of the cross shown below. You can make the cross by first drawing a

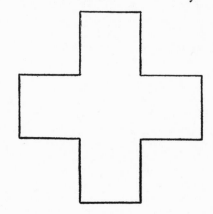

square and then attaching an equal square to each of its sides. Now make four straight cuts that divide the cross into five pieces that can be rearranged to form a square. (Answer No. 41)

The Königsberg Bridges

A river flows through the German city of Königsberg. Islands in the river are joined to the banks and to each other by seven bridges, as shown in the map below. The citizens of Königsberg, when they went out for a stroll on a Sunday afternoon, used to amuse themselves with a little game. They tried to plan their walk so that they would cross each of the seven bridges once and only once. No matter how hard they tried, they never succeeded. Finally, a mathematician named Leonhard Euler showed that they could not succeed, because it was impossible.

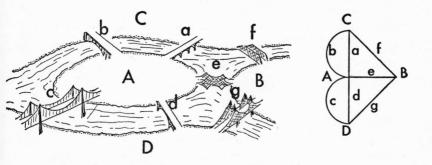

Euler first restated the problem of the bridges in simpler form. He represented each bank and each island by a dot on a piece of paper, and each bridge by a line joining the dots. The resulting figure is shown next to the map. *Then the problem was to draw the whole figure without lifting the pencil from the paper, and without retracing any lines.* By examining a lot of different figures of this type, Euler found out which ones can be drawn in this way, and which ones cannot. He noticed first that there were some dots where an even number of lines come together. He called these dots *even vertices*. There were sometimes other dots where an odd number of lines come together. He called these dots *odd vertices*. He discovered that the number of odd vertices in a figure is always even. Then he showed that you can draw a figure without lifting your pencil and without retracing a line only if the number of odd vertices in the figure is 2 or 0. If the figure has more than two odd vertices, it is impossible to do so. The figure of the Königsberg bridges has four odd vertices. That is why the citizens of Königsberg were unable to cross each bridge once and only once. When a figure has no odd vertices you can start drawing it at any point, and you end where you started. If the figure has two odd vertices, you have to start at one odd vertex, and you end at the other.

Of the three figures shown below, two can be drawn without lifting your pencil or retracing a line, while the other cannot. Find out which one cannot, and draw the two that can. Then see if you can also draw these two without lifting your pencil, without retracing any lines, *and without crossing any lines.* (Answer No. 42)

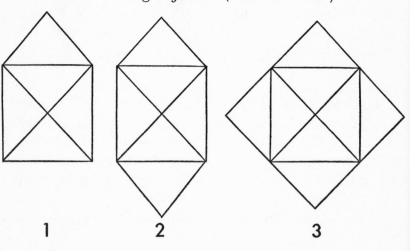

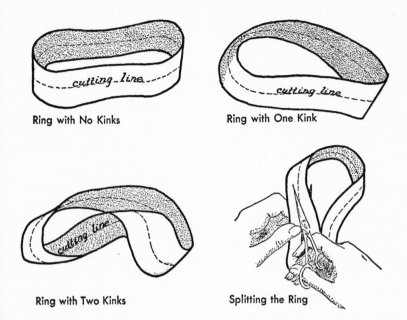

Ring with No Kinks

Ring with One Kink

Ring with Two Kinks

Splitting the Ring

Splitting the Ring

Unfold a double page of regular size newspaper and cut from the longest edge three strips of paper, each one inch wide. Bring the ends of one of the strips together to form a ring. Make sure that there are no kinks in the ring, and then fasten the ends with glue or with adhesive tape. Make a ring with the second strip, but twist one of the ends over once before fastening the ends together. Make a ring with the third piece, but give it two twists before fastening the ends together. Now, with your scissors, make a cut halfway between the edges of the first ring, and extend the cut all the way around the ring. When you finish cutting, you will have two rings that can be separated. Now make the same kind of cut around each of the other rings. What will you get as a result? Try it and get a big surprise. (Answer No. 43)

CHAPTER VI

Calculating Tricks

Multiplying in Your Head

MOST people memorize the multiplication tables only through the "twelve-times" table. If they have to multiply numbers higher than twelve, they work the example out in writing. Only a few rare number wizards can do all the long multiplications in their heads. But there are some of the longer multiplications that anybody can do in his head if he learns a few simple calculating tricks.

Numbers that end in 0. The easiest numbers to multiply are numbers that end in 0. Suppose you have to multiply 20 × 300. First disregard the zeros, and multiply the numbers that remain. Two times three gives you 6. Now, place after the 6 the number of zeros you disregarded. In this case there are three zeros, so the answer is 6,000. We can see why this trick works when we remember that our numbers are written in the ten-scale. In the ten-scale, 20 means 2 × 10, and 300 means 3 × 100. When we multiply, we get 2 × 10 × 3 × 100. When several numbers are being multiplied, you can multiply them in any order, and you will still get the same answer. So we can change the order to 2 × 3 × 10 × 100. Multiply the first two numbers first, the last two numbers next, and then multiply the results. The 2 × 3 gives us 6. The 10 × 100 gives us 1,000. Then multiplying 6 by 1,000 is like attaching three zeros to the 6.

Let's try the trick on some more examples. To multiply 70×70, write 49 followed by two zeros, so the answer is 4,900. To multiply 400×500 write 20 followed by four zeros, so the answer is 200,000. You can check these examples by multiplying them out in writing.

Numbers that end in 5. There is a special trick for multiplying by itself any number that ends in 5. First disregard the 5. Take the number that is left, and multiply it by the next higher number. Then place 25 *after* the result. For example, to multiply 65×65, first multiply 6×7, giving you 42. Then the answer is 4,225. To multiply 35×35, first multiply 3×4, giving you 12. Then the answer is 1,225. You can check these answers by doing the multiplications in writing. This trick grows out of the fact that 5 is half of ten, and our numbers are written in the ten-scale.

Numbers that differ by 2. There is a short way of multiplying numbers that differ by 2, if the number that lies between them is easy to multiply by itself. Suppose, for example, we want to multiply 19×21. The number that lies between them is 20. First multiply 20 by itself, and then subtract 1. Then the answer is 399. To multiply 29×31, first multiply 30 by itself, and then subtract 1. The answer is 899. In each case, you find the number that lies between the two multipliers, multiply it by itself, and then subtract 1.

We can see why this method works by looking at the drawing below, set up to show the example 9×11. Find-

9 x 11   (10 x 10) — 1

ing 9×11 is like counting the number of checkers in 9 rows that contain 11 checkers in each row. If we remove the last checker in each row, then there are ten checkers left in each of the nine rows. With the checkers that we removed, we can form a tenth row, but it will be incomplete. It will have one checker less than all the other rows. So the number of checkers in 9×11 checkers is one less than the number of checkers in a 10×10 square. That is why we multiply 10 by itself and then subtract 1.

Multiplying on Your Fingers

When people have trouble remembering their addition tables, they do what their ancestors did thousands of years ago. They add on their fingers. But most people don't know that you can multiply on your fingers, too. If you ever forget your multiplication tables from 6 to 10, you can use your fingers to take their place. Here is how it is done. Let each finger of each hand stand for a number from 6 to 10, as shown in the first drawing on page 71. To multiply two numbers, represent one number by the proper finger on one hand, and the other number by the proper finger on the other hand. Let these two fingers touch each other while you hold your hands with the thumbs up. Now count by tens on the fingers that touch and on those that are below them. This gives you part of your answer. To get the other part, count the number of fingers on one hand that are above the touching fingers; count the number of fingers on the other hand that are above the touching fingers; then multiply these two numbers. Add the two parts to get the final answer.

The second drawing shows the position of the fingers for multiplying 7×8. The numbers written on the lower fingers show how you use them for counting by tens. The first part of the answer is 50. Above the touching fingers, there

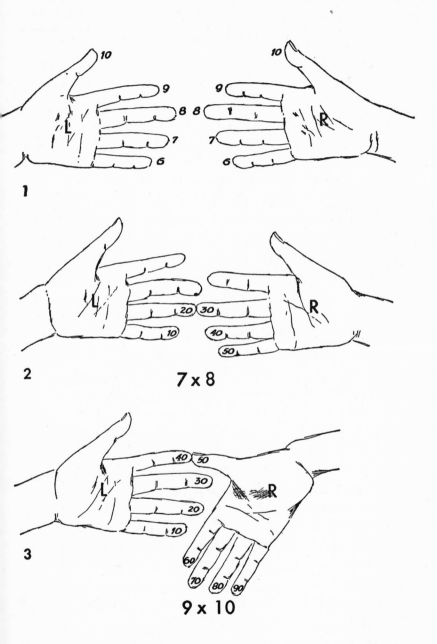

1

2　　　**7 x 8**

3　　　**9 x 10**

are 3 fingers on one hand, and 2 fingers on the other. Multiply 3×2 to get 6, the other part of the answer. Now add 50 and 6, and the result, 56, is the answer for 7×8.

The third drawing shows the position of the fingers for multiplying 9×10. Counting by tens on the lower fingers gives 90. Above the touching fingers, there is 1 finger on one hand, and 0 fingers on the other. Multiply 1×0 to get the other part of the answer, and add the product to 90.

Multiplication by Doubling

Suppose you forgot all the multiplication tables except the "two-times" table. Then you could still multiply any two numbers, no matter how large they are, as long as you know how to multiply and divide by two, and how to add. Here are the steps by which you could do it. First write the two multipliers side by side, on one line. Divide the number on the left by 2, and write the quotient that you get underneath it. Disregard any remainder that you get. Dou-

37	85	85
18	170	
9	340	340
4	680	
2	1360	
1	2720	2720
0	5440	
		3145

ble the number on the right, and write the result that you get underneath it. Now repeat this process with the two numbers you have written on the second line: divide the one on the left in half, while you double the one on the right. Keep this up until you get 0 as the quotient on the left. Cross out those lines in which the number on the left is an even number or zero. Take the numbers on the right which remain, and add them up. The result is your final answer. The example on page 72 shows the procedure for multiplying 37×85 by this method.

To see why this method works, compare the left-hand column with the procedure for writing the number 37 in the two-scale.

$$2)\overline{37}$$
$$2)\overline{18}\dots\dots\dots\dots1$$
$$2)\overline{9}\dots\dots\dots\dots0$$
$$2)\overline{4}\dots\dots\dots\dots1$$
$$2)\overline{2}\dots\dots\dots\dots0$$
$$2)\overline{1}\dots\dots\dots\dots0$$
$$0\dots\dots\dots\dots1$$

This shows that 37, written out in the two-scale, is 100,-101. This means that 37 is equal to $1 \times 32 + 0 \times 16 + 0 \times 8 + 1 \times 4 + 0 \times 2 + 1$. We can drop out the terms 0×16, 0×8, and 0×2, because each of these products is 0. Writing the other terms in reverse order, we see that 37 is equal to $1 + 4 + 32$. So to multiply 85 by 37, we can multiply 85 by 1, 4, and 32, and then add the results. The numbers to be added would be 85, 340, and 2720. The trick method of multiplication works because it is another way of writing out the same steps.

Mind-Reading Tricks

Among the most mystifying tricks of stage "magicians" are those in which they "read" other people's minds. You, too, can be a mind reader by learning the number tricks that follow.

Guessing a Birthday

To guess somebody's birthday, tell him, first, to keep in mind two numbers: the number of the month in which he was born, and the number of the day of the month on which he was born. The months are numbered in the usual way, from 1 to 12, beginning with January. Then give him these directions: "Multiply the number of the month in which you were born by 5. Add 6. Multiply by 4. Add 9. Multiply by 5. Add the number of the day on which you were born." Give him time to finish all the calculations, and, when he finishes, ask for the final result. Now you silently subtract 165 from the result. After you subtract, the last two digits tell you the day, and the other digits tell you the month of the birthday. For example, if his result is 989, when you subtract 165 you get 824. So you know he was born on the 24th day of the 8th month, that is, on August 24th. This trick is based on the fact that our numbers are written in the ten-scale. The directions you give to the person are a disguised way of adding 165, the day number, and one hundred times the month number. When you subtract 165, the day number and one hundred times the month number are left. Because the month number was multiplied by 100, it appears as the number of hundreds, so you find it to the left of the figures that represent the day number.

The Digit Struck Out

To make this trick most effective, have yourself blindfolded first. Ask someone in your audience to write down on a piece of paper or on a blackboard any three-digit number. Then tell him to reverse the order of the digits. If the result is larger than the first number, he should write it above the number. If the result is smaller, he should write it underneath the number. Then tell him to subtract. When the subtraction has been completed, ask him to multiply the result by any number he wishes. Then instruct him to strike out any one of the digits of the final answer, but not a zero. Tell him to add up the remaining digits, and *let you know what he gets*. Then *you will tell him what number he struck out*. You find out what it is mentally by simply subtracting from 9 the number he gives you. If the number he gives you has more than one digit, add them up to get one digit before you try to subtract. There is one exception to the rule. If the number he gives you is 9, then it means he crossed out a 9.

This trick is based on casting out nines. When the three-digit numbers are subtracted, the difference is a multiple of 9. When you multiply it by any other number, the product, too, comes out a multiple of 9. So the sum of the digits should be 9. If one of the digits is struck out before the others are added, the sum will be that much short of 9. That is why you can find it by subtracting from 9. Practice doing the trick by yourself before you try it with an audience.

Seeing into the Future

In this trick, you announce that you will read the future. You will add up several numbers, some provided by your audience, and some provided by you. But you will write down the answer even before you know what all the numbers are! Ask your audience to give you a three-digit number, and you write it down. Suppose the number is 473. You leave enough space for four more numbers, draw a line, and write the answer under it: 2,471. Ask your audience for a second three-digit number and write it down. *You* write the third number. Then ask for a fourth number, and *you* write the fifth number. Have your audience add the five numbers, and they will discover with amazement that the answer you wrote down is correct.

To do this trick you have to know what to write down for the answer, and what to write for the third and fifth numbers that will be added. Here are the rules. To get the answer, subtract 2 from the three-digit number you started with, and put 2 in front of the remainder. In this case, 2 from 473 leaves 471. Putting 2 in front of the 471 gives you 2,471. To get the third number, one of those that you supply, subtract the second number from 999. To get the fifth number, subtract the fourth number from 999. These subtractions are easy to do in your head. The completed example might look like the sum done below, on the left:

$$
\begin{array}{ll}
473 & 473 \\
165 & \\
834 & 1000 - 1 \\
270 & \\
\underline{729} & \underline{1000 - 1} \\
2,471 & 2,473 - 2
\end{array}
$$

The sum on the right explains why the trick works. The second and third number add up to 999, which is 1 less than 1,000. The fourth and fifth number also add up to 1 less than 1,000. So adding these four numbers to 473 is like adding 2 less than 2,000. The "2 less" explains why we subtract 2 to get 471. The "2,000" explains why we put a 2 in front of the 471.

76

Mind-Reading Cards

In this trick you use a set of five cards to help you read somebody's mind. In fact, the cards do the thinking for you. You ask a person in the audience to pick a number from 1 to 31. He may tell it to the others in the room, but not to you. Now show him card number one, and ask him if his number is on the card. If he says "yes," place the card on the table so that the word "yes," which is printed on the card, is on top. If he says "no," turn the card around so that the word "no" will be on top. Show him each of the other cards in turn, and ask him the same question. His answer tells you how to hold the card when you put it down over those that are already on the table. When all five cards are lying in a pile on the table, pick up the pile and turn it around. The number you are supposed to guess will show up through a window in the cards.

To make the cards, use the drawing on page 78 as a guide. For each card, cut a 5 inch by 5 inch square out of cardboard. Make the margins one half inch wide, and make the spaces in which the numbers are written one half inch wide and one inch long. When you are ready to cut out the windows, place one card at a time on a thick pile of newspapers, and cut along the borders of the windows with a razor or the point of a sharp knife. The windows are marked "CUT OUT" in the drawing. Notice that card number five has something written on both sides of the card. After you do the front of the card, turn it over sideways to get it in position for doing the back. Be sure that the top edge is still on top.

This trick is based on the way numbers are written in the binary scale. Card number one has on it those numbers from 1 to 31 that have the digit 1 in the first column from the right when the numbers are written in the binary scale.

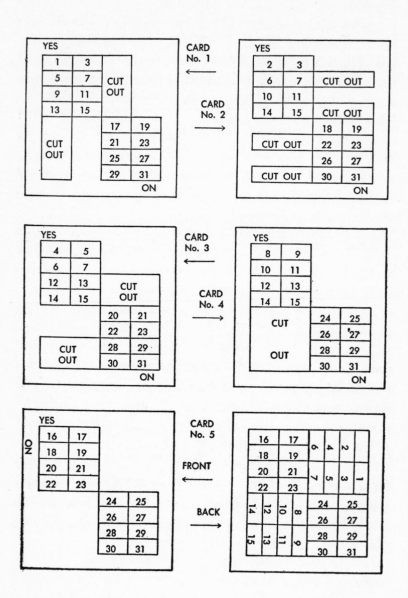

The numbers that are missing on this card are those that have the digit 0 in the first column. Card number two has on it the numbers that have the digit 1 in the second column when the number is written in the binary scale. Card number three has the numbers that have the digit 1 in the third column. Card number four has the numbers that have the digit 1 in the fourth column. The front of card number five has the numbers that have the digit 1 in the fifth column. The back of card number five has all the numbers from 1 to 31. The windows of each card are arranged so that when the word "yes" is on top, only the numbers of that card will show up through the windows. When the word "no" is on top, the numbers that are not on the card will show up. Since the words "yes" and "no" on the cards match the digits 1 and 0 column by column, each arrangement of the cards matches an arrangement of the digits, and the number that those digits represent in the binary scale is the number that shows up through the windows. For example, if the cards, in the order five, four, three, two, one, say "yes, yes, no, yes, no," then the binary number is 11,010, or 26 in the ten-scale. So the number 26 shows up through the window.

The Number in the Ashes

This is a spectacular trick in which you burn the paper on which a calculation has been done, and then produce the answer from the ashes by rubbing the ashes on your arm. Have yourself blindfolded, and give the person who will do the calculation these directions: "Write down a three-digit number so that the first and last digits differ by more than 1. Now reverse the digits. If the result is a larger number, put it on top. If the result is a smaller number, put it below. Subtract. Now reverse the digits in the answer, and add. Fold the paper twice so that the answer is hidden." After you remove the blindfold, place the paper on a metal tray and set it on fire with a match. After it burns up completely, wait a few seconds to allow the ashes to cool. Then say, "The answer *was* on the paper. Now it is in the ashes, so I shall have to get it from the ashes." Then roll up your sleeve, and rub the ashes over your arm. Like magic, the answer will appear in broad black numbers on your arm.

The secret of this trick is that, when the directions are followed, the answer always comes out 1,089. So, before you do the trick, and while no one in your audience is looking, write the number 1,089 on your arm with the edge of a wet piece of soap. The writing will dry quickly, and will be invisible. When you rub the ashes over your arm, some of it will stick to the soap film on your arm and make the numbers visible.

An April-First Trick

This is a trick you should do on April First. Give your audience the same directions for the calculation done in the last trick. The result, of course, will be 1,089, but don't let them know you know it. Continue with these additional directions: "Multiply by one million. Subtract 733,361,573. Then, under each 3 in the answer write the letter *L*. Under each 5, write the letter *O*. Under each 6, write the letter *F*. Under each 8, write the letter *I*. Under each 4, write the letter *R*. Under each 2, write the letter *P*. Under each 7, write the letter A. Then read it backward." Try it yourself, and see what it says!

CHAPTER VII

Card Tricks

THERE are two kinds of card tricks. One kind, like the typical trick of the stage magician, is done by sleight of hand. A trick like this is effective only if the performer's hands are so quick and skillful that the audience does not see what he is doing. Another kind of trick depends on the arrangement of the cards. It is really a mathematical trick that can be figured out. Doing the trick depends on knowing the secret of the arrangement of the cards, rather than on practice to develop skill with your hands. All of the tricks in this chapter are of the mathematical type.

The Josephus Ring

In the year A.D. 68, the Jewish army that was defending the town of Jotapata against the invading Romans was defeated. The commander of the army, Josephus, and some of his fellow countrymen, hid in a cave, but were later captured by the enemy. A legend has grown up about what happened in the cave, and a card trick has grown out of the legend.

According to the legend, Josephus' companions decided that they would rather die than surrender, so they proposed a suicide pact. Josephus, who, together with a friend, had secretly decided to desert to the Romans, suggested an orderly way of carrying out the suicide pact. The men were arranged in a ring, and they counted around

81

the circle. Every third man was to be killed, and the last man left was supposed to commit suicide. But Josephus made sure that his friend and he were placed so that they would be the last two left, and would remain alive.

In the Josephus-ring card trick, cards are dealt out the way Josephus' companions in the cave were selected for death. Cards are taken from the top of a deck, one at a time, and placed at the bottom of the deck, except for every third card, which is dealt out on the table. If the cards are properly arranged in the deck, the cards can be dealt out in any order you wish. Suppose, for example, you use only the thirteen cards of one suit, and you want them to be dealt out in order from ace to king. You can discover how to arrange the cards in this way: Draw thirteen spaces in a line on a piece of paper. Start with the first space, and write down a symbol for a card in every third empty space, putting them down in order from ace to king. When you reach the end of the line, return to the beginning of the line, and keep counting without interruption. When you come to spaces already filled, pass over them without counting them. Keep this up until all the spaces are filled. The arrangement you will get will be: J,5,1,8,10,2,6,Q,3,9,7,4,K. You can use the same procedure to work out the arrangement for any number of cards, to be dealt out in any order you wish.

Streets and Avenues

If a city is laid out in streets crossed by avenues, you can identify every intersection by naming the street and avenue that cross there. There is an old card trick in which you use a method as simple as all that to "guess" the card someone has picked. Although the trick is very simple, many people are mystified by it. Here is the procedure: Use only 25 cards. Have someone pick a card from the deck, look at it, and return it to the deck. Invite him to shuffle the cards. Now lay the cards on the table, face up, in five rows of five cards each. Proceed from left to right in each row, and when you finish a row, start the next row beneath it. Let the cards in the same row touch each other, but leave a space between rows. Ask your audience to point out the row that contains the chosen card. Then pick up the cards in the same order in which you put them down. Lay them out again, but this time put them down in columns of five. Proceed from top to bottom in each column, and when you finish one column start the next one to the right. However, just as before, let the cards in the same horizontal row touch each other, but leave spaces between the rows. The rows will be noticeable, but the columns will not. Once again, ask which row contains the chosen card. Then you can name the card at once, because the row that it was in before is the column that it is in now, and you find the card where its present row and column cross. For example, if it was in the third row the first time, and the fifth row the second time, then you find it in the fifth row and third column. Don't do this trick too many times for the same audience, or they will "catch on."

Three Rows

This trick uses 21 cards. Have someone pick a card, return it to the deck, and shuffle the cards. Then lay the cards out, face up, in three columns of seven cards each. Ask your audience which column contains the chosen card. Pick up the cards in each column in the order in which you put them down, but put the set of seven that includes the chosen card between the other two sets. Lay the cards out again in three columns, but this time put them into the columns in rotation, the first card in the first column, the second card in the second column, the third card in the third column, the fourth card in the first column, and so on. Again ask which column contains the chosen card. Pick them up, as before, with the chosen set of seven in the middle. Do this once again. Lay the cards out in rotation, ask which column has the card and pick up the cards again with this column in the middle. Then, if you count out the cards, the eleventh card is the one you are looking for. The explanation for this trick is simple. The first time your audience points out the column that contains the chosen card, you know the card is one of seven cards. When you lay the cards out a second time, you spread these seven cards out among three columns, so that each column has only two or three of them. When you lay the cards out a third time, you spread these two or three cards out so that each column contains only one of them, and always in the middle. By putting the chosen column in the middle the last time you pick up the cards, you automatically make the chosen card the middle card, or the eleventh.

Ten in a Line

Take ten cards, from 1 to 10, and lay them out in order starting with 1, face down, in a line, from left to right. Tell the audience that, while your back is turned, they should move some cards from the left end of the line to the right end of the line, *one card at a time.* They may move any number of cards less than ten, and you will guess how many cards they moved. Before you turn your back, you move some yourself to show how they should be moved. After the audience has made their moves, you simply pick up one of the ten cards, and *the number on the card tells how many cards were moved.* The trick, of course, is in knowing which card to pick up. This trick may be repeated many times, and the more you do it, the more mystifying it becomes, because each time you will pick up a card from a different place in the line.

Here is how you know which card to pick up: You moved some cards yourself when you were showing how the moves should be made. Count out this number of cards from the right-hand end of the line. The next card after these is the one you pick up. The number on the card tells you how many cards the audience moved. Add this number to the number of cards you moved yourself, to find out how many cards were moved altogether. When you repeat the trick, count out from the right-hand end the number of cards moved *altogether,* and pick up the next card after these. Repeat the trick as many times as you like, but keep adding the new number to the old, so that you always know how many cards were moved altogether since you first laid out the cards. Whenever the total reaches ten or more, subtract ten and keep only the remainder, so that you never have as many as ten cards to count out. Sooner or later your audience will cook up a scheme for fooling you. They will make believe they are moving cards, while they really move none at all. You will know that this has happened *when the card you pick up is the ten,* and you can foil their plot.

To understand why the trick works, do it several times with the cards face up. Then the trick will look so obvious, you will wonder why people don't see through it at once.

Turning the Square

For this trick you can use any square number of cards, like 9, 16, 25, or 49. The more cards you use, the more difficult it looks. Arrange the cards in some definite order, and remember the order. For example, with 49 cards, you might place first all the diamonds, arranged from ace to king, followed by all the clubs, then all the hearts, and finally the spades from ace to ten. In this arrangement, every card has a definite number that shows its position. For example, the two of clubs is the fifteenth card. Now lay the cards out face down in seven rows of seven cards each. Put them down row by row from left to right, starting with the top row. Now pick them up column by column, proceeding from the bottom to the top in each column, and starting with the column on the left. This obviously changes the order of the cards. Now lay the cards out again in a square the way you did before, and offer to pick out any card that is named. The secret of this trick is that the new arrangement is the same as the old arrangement, except that the whole square has been turned around 90 degrees clockwise. What used to be the top row is now the right-hand column. The old second row is now the second column from the right, and so on. Now, suppose your audience names the seven of hearts. In this arrangement the seven of hearts is the thirty-third card. So you count out 33 cards, starting in the upper right-hand corner of the square, and going down one column at a time. The thirty-third card would be the fifth card in the fifth column from the right. You turn it over, and sure enough, it is the seven of hearts. You can make this trick look more complicated by repeating the routine of laying the cards out horizontally and picking them up vertically, before you offer to pick out any card that is named. The audience will think that this leaves the cards hopelessly mixed up. But actually it does not. Doing the routine once turns the square 90 degrees, so doing it twice turns the square 180 degrees. The result is that the square is merely upside down, with the cards in each row arranged from right to left.

Nine in a Square

This trick is also based on changing the order of a set of

cards by laying them out on the table one way, and picking them up another way. Use nine cards, from 1 to 9, and lay them out in three rows of three cards each, face down. The cards will be in the positions shown below:

$$1 \quad\quad 2 \quad\quad 3$$
$$4 \quad\quad 5 \quad\quad 6$$
$$7 \quad\quad 8 \quad\quad 9$$

Then pick up the cards along diagonal lines, starting in the upper left-hand corner, and moving along each line upward to the right. This will arrange the cards in the order 1, 4, 2, 7, 5, 3, 8, 6, 9. Now lay them out again in a square the way you did before, and offer to pick out any card that is named. The secret of this trick is that three of the cards are in the same places they occupied before, and the rest of the cards moved in a very simple way. The cards that did not move are 1 (the first card), 5 (the middle card), and 9 (the last card). The other cards form a ring, and the whole ring turned clockwise so that each card moved up into the next place in the ring. The 2, for example, moved to where the 3 was, the 3 moved to where the 6 was, and so on. You can make this trick look more complicated by laying out the cards and picking them up over and over again, doing the routine more than once before you start picking out cards that are named. When you do the routine twice, the numbers in the ring move over two places clockwise. If you do it three times, they move over three places. If you do it six times, all the cards will be restored to their original places.

Ten in a Triangle

Ten is a triangular number, so ten cards can be arranged in a triangle as shown on the next page:

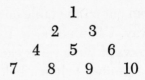

After laying the cards out face down in this way, pick them up along the diagonal lines, starting in the lower left-hand corner. This puts the cards in the order 7, 4, 2, 1, 8, 5, 3, 9, 6, 10. Then lay them out again in a triangle the way you did before, and offer to pick out any card that is named. Now let us figure out an easy way of keeping track of where the cards are in the new arrangement. Write down on a piece of paper the number 1, to stand for the first card. In the new arrangement, the 1 is the fourth card, so write 4 after the 1. In the new arrangement, the 4 is the second card, so write 2 after the 4. In the new arrangement, the 2 is the third card, so write 3 after the 2. In the new arrangement, the 3 is the seventh card, so write 7 after the 3. In the new arrangement, the 7 is the first card. But 1 is the first number we wrote down, so now just put parentheses around the whole set of numbers, and the set will look like this: (14237). A set like this is called a *cycle*, if we think of the numbers as being arranged in a ring, so that the 7 is followed by the 1. The secret of the trick is that when the cards are rearranged, you can find the new position of any card in the cycle by looking at the number next to it on the right. So, if you *memorize the cycle*, you will know that the 1 will be in the fourth place, the 4 will be in the second place, and so on. By the same procedure we find that there is another cycle, (5698), which you should memorize, too. Notice, too, that the tenth card doesn't change its place at all. To make this trick look more complicated, do what was suggested in the last two tricks. Put the cards down and pick them up over and over again,.

doing the routine more than once. When you do it twice, the new position of a card is shown by the number two places to the right in its cycle. When you do it three times, the new position is shown by the number three places to the right, and so on. In this case you would have to do it twenty times to get all the cards back to their original positions.

Make Up Your Own

The last three tricks are homemade tricks, made up by the author. You can make up your own card tricks, too. To make up a card trick, lay the cards out in some definite arrangement, and then pick them up in some other definite order. Write down the new arrangement of the cards on a piece of paper. Then, as we did in the last trick, figure out the cycles that show how the cards change places in groups. Memorize the cycles, and you are ready to perform your trick.

CHAPTER VIII

Games for One

THE games in this chapter may be used as rainy-day games, when you are indoors, alone, with nothing else to do. But they are also good as party games. It is fun to challenge other people to play them, and watch them while they try. The object of each game is to reach a certain goal while playing the game according to the rules.

Four Fours

This is a paper-and-pencil game. The object of the game is to combine four fours with any other mathematical symbols except numbers, to produce every whole number from 1 to 20.

For example, $\dfrac{4+4}{4+4} = 1; \quad \dfrac{4 \times 4}{4+4} = 2; \quad \dfrac{4+4+4}{4} = 3.$

You may use the symbols for addition, subtraction, multiplication, and division. You may also use the square-root symbol, and the decimal point. You may use up some of the fours by putting them side by side to write a number in the ten-scale, like 44. You may also use 4 as a power. This means writing it near the upper right-hand corner of a number in the kind of shorthand we used to write square and cubic numbers. Just as 4^2 (read as four square) means 4×4, and 4^3 (read as four cube) means $4 \times 4 \times 4$, 4^4 (read as four to the fourth power) means $4 \times 4 \times 4 \times 4$, and 1^4 (read as one to the fourth power) means $1 \times 1 \times 1 \times 1$.

Now see how many of the numbers you can get without any help.

Towers of Hanoi

To make the equipment for this game, cut out eight cardboard circles, all of different sizes. Drill three holes in a board so that the distance between holes is greater than the width of the widest circle. Glue an upright dowel into each hole. In each circle, cut a hole at the center, wide enough to fit over a dowel. Then place all the cardboard discs on one dowel, in order of size, with the largest one at the bottom. This arrangement of the discs is called a *tower*. The object of the game is to move the entire tower from one dowel to another, in the smallest possible number of moves. Each move consists of moving a disc from one dowel to one of the other two. Meanwhile, these rules must be observed: 1) *Move only one disc at a time;* 2) *Never put a large disc on top of a smaller disc.* If you don't want to take the trouble to cut out circles and glue dowels into a board, you can make a simplified set by cutting out eight squares of different sizes, and resting them on three plates instead of on dowels. In any case, be sure to observe the rules as you play the game.

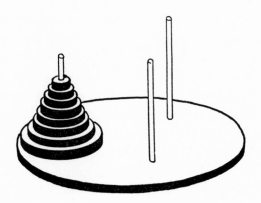

To become familiar with the way the game works, try it first with only 3 discs. You should be able to transfer a tower of 3 discs in 7 moves. Then try it with 4 discs. To move the tower of 4 discs, first you use 7 moves to transfer the 3 top discs to one of the other two dowels. This frees the bottom disc, and you move it to the vacant dowel. Then it will take 7 more moves to get the other three discs back on top of it. So the number of moves required altogether is 15. When you play the game with 5 discs you have to move the top four discs twice,—once to free the bottom disc, and once to get them back on the bottom disc, after the bottom disc has been moved. So moving 5 discs takes 31 moves. Moving 6 discs takes 63 moves; moving 7 discs takes 127 moves; and *moving 8 discs takes 255 moves.*

For lazy people who don't want to try to figure the game out for themselves, there is a way of letting *numbers* tell you how to make the right moves. In your mind, number the discs from 1 to 8 according to size, from the smallest to the largest. Also, number the moves in the game from first to last, using the numbers from 1 to 255. Write down the numbers of the moves in *the binary scale,* as you go on from each move to the next. To find out what disc to transfer at each move, and where to place it, look at the binary-scale number that belongs to that move. Count the digits from the *right* until you reach the first digit that is a 1. The number of digits you counted tells you which disc to move. For example, if the first 1 from the right is the third digit, then you move the third disc. Now you have to find out where to place it. If there are no other digits to the left of the first 1, then you place the disc on the dowel that has no discs on it. If there are other digits to the left of the first 1, you count digits from the right again until you reach the second 1. The number of digits you count this time identifies a larger disc that was moved before. You must decide whether to put the disc you are moving on top of this larger disc, or not on it, in which case you put it on the dowel where the larger disc isn't. To decide this question, you count the number of zeros between the first 1 from the right and the second 1 from the right. If there are no zeros between them, or an even number of zeros between them, you put the disc that you are moving *on* the disc that the second 1 refers to. If the number of zeros between them is odd, you put the disc *not on* it.

For example, here are the numbers from 1 to 15, written in the binary scale. Alongside them are the instructions they give for the first fifteen moves:

1	Move disc 1.
10	Move disc 2.
11	Place disc 1 on disc 2.
100	Move disc 3.
101	Place disc 1 not on disc 3.
110	Place disc 2 on disc 3.
111	Place disc 1 on disc 2.
1,000	Move disc 4.
1,001	Place disc 1 on disc 4.
1,010	Place disc 2 not on disc 4.
1,011	Place disc 1 on disc 2.
1,100	Place disc 3 on disc 4.
1,101	Place disc 1 not on disc 3.
1,110	Place disc 2 on disc 3.
1,111	Place disc 1 on disc 2.

The mathematician who invented this game made up an interesting little story about it. He said that in a temple in Benares there are three diamond needles mounted on a brass plate. When God created the world, he put sixty-four golden discs on one of the needles, in order of size, with the largest on bottom. The priests in the temple now work day and night moving the discs from one needle to another according to the divine laws, which require that they move only one disc at a time, and never put a large disc on a smaller one. When they finish moving the whole tower of sixty-four discs, the world will come to an end. If you are worried that this may happen before you get a chance to go to that ball game you wanted to see, you may set your mind at rest. To move a tower of sixty-four discs would take 18,446,744,073,709,551,615 moves. If each move takes one second, it would take the priests more than 500,000 million years to finish the job.

Chinese Rings

To make the equipment for this game, you need eight brass curtain rings, eight pieces of stiff wire each about seven inches long, one piece of stiff wire about twenty-four inches long, a strip of wood that is one inch wide, one-half inch thick, and about ten inches long, and a three-inch piece of broomstick. The wire may be cut from common wire clothes hangers. First bend the twenty-four-inch wire to form a long, narrow loop, just wide enough for the rings to fit over it. With pliers, twist the ends of the wire together to close the loop. Drill a hole in the end of the piece of broomstick, and force the twisted ends of the loop into it, to give the loop a wooden handle. Drill eight holes in the strip of one-inch wood. Make each hole just wide enough for a wire to pass through. Make the spaces between the holes as big as the width of the rings. Attach each of the seven-inch wires to one of the rings by twisting one end of the wire around it two or three times. Now the parts are ready to be assembled. Hold the wire loop so that its wooden handle is on the left, as shown in the drawing. Place the strip of wood a few inches under it. To place the first ring on the loop, insert its wire through the loop from above, and then slip the ring onto the loop from the right. Then insert the end of the wire through the first hole on

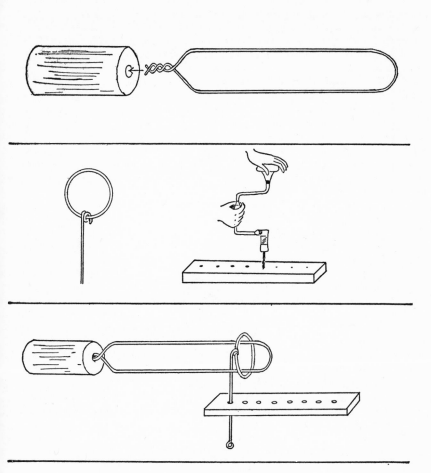

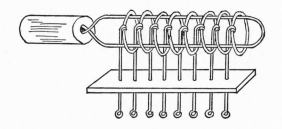

the left in the wooden strip. Bend the end of the wire into a small loop so that it cannot be pulled back again. Insert the wire of the second ring through the loop *and through the first ring,* and then slip the ring onto the loop. Pass the end of the wire through the second hole in the wooden strip, and then bend it into a small loop. Repeat the same procedure with each new ring that you put on. Be sure that the wire of each ring passes through both the loop and the ring before it, passes through the next hole in the strip of wood, and is held in place by a small loop at its end. When all the rings are on the big loop, you are ready to play the game.

The object of the game is to remove all the rings from the loop without untwisting the wires. You can remove a ring from the loop by slipping it off the end at the right, and then dropping it through the loop from above. When you try it, you will discover that that is more easily said than done, because you can remove a ring *only when the ring immediately to the right of it is still on the loop while all the others to the right of it are off the loop.* This complicates matters in two ways. First, it makes it necessary to remove the rings in a definite order. Secondly, once a ring is off, it doesn't stay off all the time. You may have to put it back on to get another ring off. To put a ring back on, you pass it through the loop from below, and then slip it onto the loop at the right-hand end. With this information to help you, you should be able to work out the rest of the puzzle by yourself. After the rings have all been removed from the loop, you can put them back on by going through all the steps again in reverse order.

For the lazy (or for the curious), there is a way of doing this puzzle with the help of numbers written in the binary scale. We represent each possible arrangement of the rings by an eight-digit number in the binary scale in this way: Each digit belongs to a ring, and the rings and digits are lined up in the same order. If the ring on the extreme left is on the loop, its digit is 1. If it is off the loop, its digit is 0. For all the other rings, when the ring is off, its digit is the same as the digit to the left of it. If the ring is on, its digit is different from the digit to the left of it. So, as you scan the digits from left to right, if a digit is a repeat, then its ring is off, but if the digit is a change from the digit to the left of it, the ring is on. When all the rings are on, the arrangement is represented by the number 10101010. To get directions for removing the rings, count backward from this number by subtracting 1 at a time, using the rules of the binary scale. By comparing the arrangement of the rings that belongs to each number with the arrangement that belongs to the next lower number you can see which ring has to be moved. We start with the number 10101010, which means that the rings are in this position: ON, ON, ON, ON, ON, ON, ON, ON. When we subtract 1 we get 10101001, which means that the second position of the rings is: ON, ON, ON, ON, ON, ON, OFF, ON. Comparing this with the first position, we see that to get the second position we must *take the second ring off,* (counting the rings from the right). This is the first move. Now subtract 1 again, and we get 10101000, which means that the third position of the rings is: ON, ON, ON, ON, ON, ON, OFF, OFF. Comparing this with the second position, we see that to get the third position we must *take the first ring off.* This is the second move. The table below shows the next ten numbers, the positions they describe, and the moves they tell us to make:

10100111	ON, ON, ON, ON, OFF, ON, OFF, OFF	4th ring off
10100110	ON, ON, ON, ON, OFF, ON, OFF, ON	1st ring on
10100101	ON, ON, ON, ON, OFF, ON, ON, ON	2nd ring on
10100100	ON, ON, ON, ON, OFF, ON, ON, OFF	1st ring off
10100011	ON, ON, ON, ON, OFF, OFF, ON, OFF	3rd ring off
10100010	ON, ON, ON, ON, OFF, OFF, ON, ON	1st ring on

10100001 ON, ON, ON, ON, OFF, OFF, OFF, ON   2nd ring off
10100000 ON, ON, ON, ON, OFF, OFF, OFF, OFF   1st ring off
10011111 ON, ON, OFF, ON, OFF, OFF, OFF, OFF   6th ring off
10011110 ON, ON, OFF, ON, OFF, OFF, OFF, ON   1st ring on

Keep it up until you get the number 00000000, for the position OFF, OFF, OFF, OFF, OFF, OFF, OFF, OFF.

To put the rings back on the loop, start with the number 00000000, and then add 1 for each move. The first five moves are shown below:

00000001 OFF, OFF, OFF, OFF, OFF, OFF, OFF, ON 1st ring on
00000010 OFF, OFF, OFF, OFF, OFF, OFF, ON, ON   2nd ring on
00000011 OFF, OFF, OFF, OFF, OFF, OFF, ON, OFF 1st ring off
00000100 OFF, OFF, OFF, OFF, OFF, ON, ON, OFF   3rd ring on
00000101 OFF, OFF, OFF, OFF, OFF, ON, ON, ON   1st ring on

Keep this up until you get the number 10101010, for the position ON, ON, ON, ON, ON, ON, ON, ON.

CHAPTER IX

Games for Two

The Gambler's Dream

EVERY gambler dreams of working out a system of playing that will guarantee that he will win. In games of chance this is a false hope. But there are some games where the gambler's dream has come true. In the first two games of this chapter there is really a winning system. If you know the system, and your opponent does not, then you can always win.

One to Twenty

This game is a simple counting contest. Two people count from 1 to 20. They take turns at counting, and count either one or two numbers in a row at each turn, starting where the other person left off. The one who reaches 20 wins. After you play this game for a while, you discover that you are sure to win if you manage to reach 17. Because, if you end your turn on the number 17, then, if your opponent counts one number after that, you count two, and if he counts two numbers, you count one. In either case, you end on 20 and win the game. It works out this way because 17 is three below 20. Count back by threes and you get a set of special numbers, 14, 11, 8, 5, and 2. If you end a turn on any one of these numbers, you can be sure to reach the higher ones of this set, and then reach 17 and 20. So here is the winning system: If you have the first turn, start by saying, "One, two." Then, after that, when your opponent says one number, you respond by saying two numbers; and when your opponent says two numbers, you respond by saying one number. In this way you climb up the number steps three steps at a time, stopping at 5, 8, 11, 14, 17, and 20. If your opponent has the first turn, try as early as you can to end one of your turns on one of the numbers 2, 5, 8, 11, 14, 17 and 20. However, if your opponent has the first turn, and *he* knows the winning system, then you are sure to lose.

Nim

The game of Nim may be played with sticks, pebbles, coins, or any other small objects. Let us describe the game as played with coins. The coins are arranged in three lines with any number of coins in each line. The two players take turns at making their moves. A move consists of taking away coins according to these rules: In each move you may take away coins from only one line. You may take away as many coins as you wish, but you must take away at least one. You may take away a whole line if you want to. The player who takes away the last coin wins.

The winning system for this game depends on expressing the number of coins in each line in the binary scale. This is like noticing which of the numbers 1, 2, 4, 8, 16, and so on, have to be added to get that number. For example, suppose you start the game with 9 coins in the first line, 10 coins in the second line, and 11 coins in the third line. Nine is the sum of 8 and 1. Ten is the sum of 8 and 2. Eleven is the sum of 8 and 2 and 1. This information is summarized in the table below, where a column is provided for each of the numbers 1, 2, 4, and 8. A column is left blank when the number is not used. The same information is written more briefly in the binary numbers to the right of the table. The digits in the binary numbers refer to the numbers 8, 4, 2, and 1, in that order. The digit 1 means the number is being used. The digit 0 means the number is not being used.

Eights	Fours	Twos	Ones	Binary Number
8			1	1001
8		2		1010
8		2	1	1011

If we count the number of entries in each column, we get the numbers 3, 0, 2, 2, showing how many eights, fours, twos and ones are used altogether. We get the same figures if we count the number of ones in each column in the three binary numbers at the right. Notice that one of these figures is an odd number, 3. For this reason we call the set of numbers (9, 10, 11) an *odd combination*. Now suppose the player who makes the first move takes eight coins away from the third row. Then the new combination looks like this:

Eights	Fours	Twos	Ones	Binary Number
8			1	1001
8		2		1010
		2	1	0011

The number of entries in each column now is 2, 0, 2, 2. Notice that each of these figures is an even number. For this reason we call the set of numbers (9, 10, 3) an *even combination*. A combination is called even if the number of entries in every column is even. A combination is called odd if the number of entries in one or more columns is odd. *The secret of the winning system is to choose your move so that it results in an even combination.* This is always possible if the combination before you make your move is odd. It is not possible if the combination before you make your move is even. But if your opponent does not know the system, sooner or later he will make a move that gives you an odd combination. Then your next move can make it even, and you are on your way to winning the game.

To show how the winning system is applied, let us play out a full game, starting with the coins arranged in three lines to give the set of numbers (9, 10, 11). We have already seen that the first player can turn this into an even combination by removing eight coins from the last row. The numbers after this move are (9, 10, 3). Now suppose his opponent takes away 4 coins from the first line. The result is shown below:

EIGHTS	FOURS	TWOS	ONES	BINARY NUMBER
	4		1	0101
8		2		1010
		2	1	0011

There is an odd number of entries in the eights column, and also in the fours column. If the first player wants to use the winning system, he must choose his move so that it changes the number of entries in each of these columns to an even number. He cannot remove both the 8 and the 4, because they are in different lines, and he can remove coins from only one line. What he has to do then is work on the line that contains the higher of the two numbers, the 8. But he does not remove all of the 8. He removes only 4 coins from the second line. The other four coins raise the number of entries in the fours column to two, and the result is an even combination, as shown below:

EIGHTS	FOURS	TWOS	ONES	BINARY NUMBER
	4		1	0101
	4	2		0110
		2	1	0011

102

If his opponent next removes three coins from the first line, the new combination is:

Eights	Fours	Twos	Ones	Binary Number
		2		0010
	4	2		0110
		2	1	0011

Now three of the columns have an odd number of entries. The first player can remove the 4 and the 2 in the second line, but he cannot remove a 1, because there is no 1 in the second line. What he has to do, then, is put another 1 in. So, for his answering move, he must take five coins away from the second line, with this result:

Eights	Fours	Twos	Ones	Binary Number
		2		0010
			1	0001
		2	1	0011

If his opponent removes one coin from the first line, the result is:

Eights	Fours	Twos	Ones	Binary Number
			1	0001
			1	0001
		2	1	0011

To answer this move he takes away all the coins in the third line. This leaves one coin each in the first and second lines. His opponent, in his next move, can remove only one of them, so the first player will remove the last one, and win.

Oware

Oware (pronounced o-wah'-ruh) is an exciting game played by the people of the Gold Coast in West Africa. To play the game you need 48 counters, and a board divided into 12 compartments. To make the board, get a piece of wood 24 inches long and 12 inches wide. Nail a strip of half-round molding down the middle of the board to divide it in half. Then, with smaller strips of molding, divide each half of the board into six compartments, as shown in

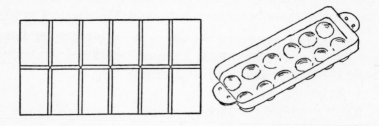

the drawing. For the counters, pick up 48 smooth pebbles the next time you are at the beach. If you wish, you can use pennies instead of pebbles, and a plastic egg holder instead of the board.

Each side, consisting of six compartments, belongs to one of the two players. The game begins with four pebbles in each compartment. The players take turns at making their moves. All moves are made in the same direction, counterclockwise around the board. When a player makes a move, he takes all the pebbles out of one of the compartments on his side, and then, as he moves his hand around the board counterclockwise, puts one pebble into each compartment as he passes over it. In later stages of the game he may find twelve or more pebbles in a compartment. When he moves them, he will have enough to go completely around the board and come back to the compartment from which he took them. But in that case,

Case 1
Before

B6 B5 B4 B3 B2 B1

A1 A2 A3 A4 A5 A6

After

B6 B5 B4 B3 B2 B1

A1 A2 A3 A4 A5 A6

Case 2
Before

B6 B5 B4 B3 B2 B1

A1 A2 A3 A4 A5 A6.

After

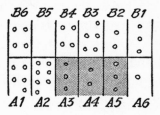

B6 B5 B4 B3 B2 B1

A1 A2 A3 A4 A5 A6

Case 3
Before

B6 B5 B4 B3 B2 B1

A1 A2 A3 A4 A5 A6

After

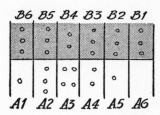

B6 B5 B4 B3 B2 B1

A1 A2 A3 A4 A5 A6

he does not put a pebble into the compartment that he has just emptied. He skips over that compartment and continues to put one pebble into each of the others, in order. The object of the game is to make captures. A player makes a capture when the last pebble he puts down is on his opponent's side, and raises the total number of pebbles in that compartment to 2 or 3. When this happens, he removes all the pebbles in that compartment and puts them aside as his winnings. If the last pebble put down makes no capture, then no captures are made at all. But if the last pebble put down does make a capture, then it starts a chain reaction going backward. Then the next-to-the-last pebble put down can also capture, if it, too, is on the opponent's side, and if it raises the total in the compartment to 2 or 3. The one before that may also capture in the same way, and so on. But the chain of captures is broken as soon as a compartment is reached that contains more than three pebbles or less than two. The chain also ends when the end of the opponent's side is reached, because a player does not make captures on his own side.

The game can end in three ways: 1) It ends when no more pebbles are left on the board. 2) It ends when a player has to move, but has no pebbles on his side with which to move. In that case, the player who still has pebbles keeps them as part of his winnings. 3) It ends when there are so few pieces left that it is obvious that the two players will be chasing each other around the board forever without making any more captures. If the two players agree that this is the case, they divide up the pebbles on the board. The player who has won the most pebbles wins the game.

To show some typical moves, let us watch two players, A and B, as they play a game. The compartments on A's side are labeled A1, A2, A3, A4, A5, A6. The compartments on B's side are labeled B1, B2, B3, B4, B5, B6. Three moves are shown in different stages of the game. In each case the diagram shows the board before and after the move.

In the first diagram, the game has just begun. A has made the opening move by taking pebbles out of compartment A3, and putting one each into A4, A5, A6, and B1. No captures were made.

In the second diagram, B takes the pebbles out of compartment B5, and puts one each into B6, A1, A2, A3, A4, and A5. He makes captures in A5, A4, and A3, and removes the pebbles in those compartments from the board.

In the third diagram, A has been accumulating pebbles in compartment A6. Now the moment he has been waiting for has arrived. He has 17 pebbles in A6, and it is his move. He takes the 17 pebbles out of A6, and puts them into the other compartments, one at a time, in this order: B1, B2, B3, B4, B5, B6, A1, A2, A3, A4, A5, B1, B2, B3, B4, B5, B6. He captures in every compartment on B's side. B has no more pebbles left with which to move, and the game is over.

ANSWERS TO PROBLEMS
AND PUZZLES

Answers to Problems and Puzzles

1. *Counting by ones:* The open steps go up one at a time. The first nine hidden steps are the same as the open steps. The tenth number in the open steps is 10. Its remainder, when we divide by nine, is 1. Since the open steps continue to go up one at a time, the hidden steps do, too. That is why the numbers from 1 to 9 are repeated in the hidden steps.

Counting by threes: The open steps go up three at a time, so the hidden steps do, too. The fourth number in the open steps is 12. Its remainder, when we divide by nine, is 3. So the hidden steps repeat the numbers 3, 6, 9.

Counting by fives: The open steps go up five at a time. If we go up the steps *two steps at a time* by skipping every other step, then the increase is 10 at a time. But when we divide 10 by 9, the remainder is 1. So, if we start with the first of the hidden steps and then skip every other step, we get a series of numbers that go up 1 at a time. If we start with the second step and then skip every other step, we get the other series of numbers going up 1 at a time. That is why the hidden steps are made up of two sets of steps that are interlocked.

Counting by sixes: The open steps go up six at a time. But six is 3 below 9. So the hidden steps go down 3 at a time. The next step is 6 below a multiple of 9. That is why the remainder is 3. The third step is 9 below a multiple of nine, so it is itself a multiple of 9, and the remainder is nine. Since the remainders go down three at a time, the numbers 9, 6, 3 are repeated in the hidden steps.

Counting by sevens: The open steps go up seven at a time. But seven is 2 below nine. So the hidden steps go down 2 at a time. That is why the first hidden steps are 7, 5, 3, 1. A number that has a remainder of 1 is 1 above a multiple of nine, so it is also 10 above a multiple of nine. Continuing along the hidden steps by going down 2 at a time, the next remainder would be 8. That is why the next hidden steps are the even numbers 8, 6, 4, 2. The next hidden step after 2 would be a remainder of 0, which is the same as a remainder of 9. So the odd numbers begin to appear all over again.

Counting by nines: All the numbers in the open steps are multiples of nine, so the remainders are all 9. That is why the hidden steps stay in one place.

2. $3 \times 8 + 6 = 30;$ $2 \times 64 + 1 \times 8 + 5 = 141;$ $6 \times 8 + 4 = 52;$
    $4 \times 64 + 2 \times 8 = 272.$

3. EIGHT-SCALE:

$$\begin{array}{r} 32 \\ + 14 \\ \hline 46 \end{array}$$

$$\begin{array}{r} 65 \\ + 24 \\ \hline 111 \end{array}$$

$$\begin{array}{r} 113 \\ + 51 \\ \hline 164 \end{array}$$

$$\begin{array}{r} 235 \\ + 154 \\ \hline 411 \end{array}$$

$$\begin{array}{r} 77 \\ + 77 \\ \hline 176 \end{array}$$

TEN-SCALE:

$3 \times 8 + 2 = 26$
$1 \times 8 + 4 = 12$
$4 \times 8 + 6 = 38$

$6 \times 8 + 5 = 53$
$2 \times 8 + 4 = 20$
$1 \times 64 + 1 \times 8 + 1 = 73$

$1 \times 64 + 1 \times 8 + 3 = 75$
$5 \times 8 + 1 = 41$
$1 \times 64 + 6 \times 8 + 4 = 116$

$2 \times 64 + 3 \times 8 + 5 = 157$
$1 \times 64 + 5 \times 8 + 4 = 108$
$4 \times 64 + 1 \times 8 + 1 = 265$

$7 \times 8 + 7 = 63$
$7 \times 8 + 7 = 63$
$1 \times 64 + 7 \times 8 + 6 = 126$

4. EIGHT-SCALE:

$$\begin{array}{r} 17 \\ \times 42 \\ \hline 36 \\ 74 \\ \hline 776 \end{array}$$

TEN-SCALE:

$1 \times 8 + 7 = 15$
$4 \times 8 + 2 = 34$
$\qquad \qquad 60$
$\qquad \qquad 45$
$7 \times 64 + 7 \times 8 + 6 = 510$

112

$$
\begin{array}{r}
106 \\
\times\ 45 \\
\hline
536 \\
430 \\
\hline
5036
\end{array}
$$

$$1\times64+0\times8+6=70$$
$$4\times8+5=37$$
$$\overline{490}$$
$$210$$
$$5\times512+0\times64+3\times8+6=\overline{2590}$$

$$
\begin{array}{r}
13 \\
\times\,31 \\
\hline
13 \\
41 \\
\hline
423
\end{array}
$$

$$1\times8+3=11$$
$$3\times8+1=25$$
$$\overline{55}$$
$$22$$
$$4\times64+2\times8+3=\overline{275}$$

5. $8\,\overline{)\,53}$
    $8\,\overline{)\,6}\ldots\ldots\ldots\ldots 5$
    $0\ldots\ldots\ldots\ldots 6$ Answer: 65.

$8\,\overline{)\,154}$
$8\,\overline{)\,19}\ldots\ldots\ldots 2$
$8\,\overline{)\,2}\ldots\ldots\ldots 3$
$0\ldots\ldots\ldots 2$ Answer: 232.

$8\,\overline{)\,1067}$
$8\,\overline{)\,133}\ldots\ldots\ldots 3$
$8\,\overline{)\,16}\ldots\ldots\ldots 5$
$8\,\overline{)\,2}\ldots\ldots\ldots 0$
$0\ldots\ldots\ldots 2$ Answer: 2,053.

6. $1\times144+10\times12+3=267;$ $5\times144+2\times12+4=748;$
    $1\times12+9=21;$ $10\times144+11\times12+10=1582;$
    $2\times144+0\times12+11=299.$

7. $12\,\overline{)\,1769}$
    $12\,\overline{)\,147}\ldots\ldots\ldots 5$
    $12\,\overline{)\,12}\ldots\ldots\ldots 3$
    $12\,\overline{)\,1}\ldots\ldots\ldots 0$
    $0\ldots\ldots\ldots 1$ Answer: 1,035.

113

$$12 \overline{)\,310}$$
$$12 \overline{)\,25} \ldots \ldots \ldots \text{T}$$
$$12 \overline{)\,2} \ldots \ldots \ldots 1$$
$$0 \ldots \ldots \ldots 2 \qquad \text{Answer: 21T.}$$

$$12 \overline{)\,1596}$$
$$12 \overline{)\,133} \ldots \ldots \ldots 0$$
$$12 \overline{)\,11} \ldots \ldots \ldots 1$$
$$0 \ldots \ldots \ldots \text{E} \qquad \text{Answer: E10.}$$

8.

TWELVE-SCALE:	TEN-SCALE:

58	$5 \times 12 + 8 = 68$
$+ 14$	$1 \times 12 + 4 = 16$
70	$7 \times 12 + 0 = 84$

27	$2 \times 12 + 7 = 31$
$+ 1E$	$1 \times 12 + 11 = 23$
46	$4 \times 12 + 6 = 54$

T1T	$10 \times 144 + 1 \times 12 + 10 = 1462$
$+ \ 1ET$	$1 \times 144 + 11 \times 12 + 10 = \ \ 286$
1018	$1 \times 1728 + 0 \times 144 + 1 \times 12 + 8 = 1748$

43	$4 \times 12 + 3 = 51$
$+ 58$	$5 \times 12 + 8 = 68$
9E	$9 \times 12 + 11 = 119$

68	$6 \times 12 + 8 = 80$
$+ 19$	$1 \times 12 + 9 = 21$
85	$8 \times 12 + 5 = 101$

9.

TWELVE-SCALE:	TEN-SCALE:

123	$1 \times 144 + 2 \times 12 + 3 = 171$
$\times TE$	$10 \times 12 + 11 = 131$
1109	171
ET6	513
10E69	171

$$1 \times 20736 + 0 \times 1728 + 11 \times 144 + 6 \times 12 + 9 = \overline{22401}$$

114

$$
\begin{array}{r}
87 \\
\times 45 \\
\hline
36E \\
2T4 \\
\hline
31TE
\end{array}
\qquad
\begin{array}{r}
8 \times 12 + 7 = 103 \\
4 \times 12 + 5 = 53 \\
\hline
309 \\
515 \\
\hline
3 \times 1728 + 1 \times 144 + 10 \times 12 + 11 = 5459
\end{array}
$$

$$
\begin{array}{r}
34 \\
\times 80 \\
\hline
2280
\end{array}
\qquad
\begin{array}{r}
3 \times 12 + 4 = 40 \\
8 \times 12 + 0 = 96 \\
\hline
240 \\
360 \\
\hline
2 \times 1728 + 2 \times 144 + 8 \times 12 + 0 = 3840
\end{array}
$$

10. $1 \times 4 + 0 \times 2 + 0 = 4;$ $\quad 1 \times 4 + 0 \times 2 + 1 = 5;$
    $1 \times 4 + 1 \times 2 + 0 = 6;$ $\quad 1 \times 8 + 0 \times 4 + 1 \times 2 + 0 = 10;$
    $1 \times 8 + 1 \times 4 + 1 \times 2 + 1 = 15.$

11.
```
2) 35
2) 17..............1
 2) 8..............1
 2) 4..............0
 2) 2..............0
 2) 1..............0
   0..............1     Answer: 100,011.
```

```
2) 7
2) 3..............1
2) 1..............1
  0..............1     Answer: 111.
```

```
2) 83
2) 41..............1
2) 20..............1
2) 10..............0
 2) 5..............0
 2) 2..............1
 2) 1..............0
   0..............1     Answer: 1,010,011.
```

115

$$2 \overline{)\ 10}$$
$$2 \overline{)\ 5} \ldots\ldots\ldots\ldots 0$$
$$2 \overline{)\ 2} \ldots\ldots\ldots\ldots 1$$
$$2 \overline{)\ 1} \ldots\ldots\ldots\ldots 0$$
$$0 \ldots\ldots\ldots\ldots 1 \qquad \text{Answer: 1,010.}$$

$$2 \overline{)\ 5}$$
$$2 \overline{)\ 2} \ldots\ldots\ldots\ldots 1$$
$$2 \overline{)\ 1} \ldots\ldots\ldots\ldots 0$$
$$0 \ldots\ldots\ldots\ldots 1 \qquad \text{Answer: 101.}$$

12.

1000	1001	1010	1011	1100	1101
+ 1	+ 1	+ 1	+ 1	+ 1	+ 1
1001	1010	1011	1100	1101	1110

1110	1111
+ 1	+ 1
1111	10000

13.

TWO-SCALE:

TEN-SCALE:

$$
\begin{array}{r}
101 \\
+ 110 \\
\hline
1011
\end{array}
\qquad
\begin{array}{r}
1\times4+0\times2+1=\ 5 \\
1\times4+1\times2+0=\ 6 \\
\hline
1\times8+0\times4+1\times2+1=11
\end{array}
$$

$$
\begin{array}{r}
11 \\
+ 10 \\
\hline
101
\end{array}
\qquad
\begin{array}{r}
1\times2+1=3 \\
1\times2+0=2 \\
\hline
1\times4+0\times2+1=5
\end{array}
$$

$$
\begin{array}{r}
11 \\
+ 11 \\
\hline
110
\end{array}
\qquad
\begin{array}{r}
1\times2+1=3 \\
1\times2+1=3 \\
\hline
1\times4+1\times2+0=6
\end{array}
$$

$$
\begin{array}{r}
10101 \\
+ 1010 \\
\hline
11111
\end{array}
\qquad
\begin{array}{r}
1\times16+0\times8+1\times4+0\times2+1=21 \\
1\times8+0\times4+1\times2+0=10 \\
\hline
1\times16+1\times8+1\times4+1\times2+1=31
\end{array}
$$

$$
\begin{array}{r}
111 \\
+ 11 \\
\hline
1010
\end{array}
\qquad
\begin{array}{r}
1\times4+1\times2+1=\ 7 \\
1\times2+1=\ 3 \\
\hline
1\times8+0\times4+1\times2+0=10
\end{array}
$$

116

14. Two-Scale: Ten-Scale:

$$
\begin{array}{r}
101 \\
\times\ 10 \\
\hline
1010
\end{array}
\qquad
\begin{array}{r}
1\times4+0\times2+1=\ 5 \\
1\times2+0=\ 2 \\
\hline
1\times8+0\times4+1\times2+0=10
\end{array}
$$

$$
\begin{array}{r}
111 \\
\times\ 11 \\
\hline
111 \\
111 \\
\hline
10101
\end{array}
\qquad
\begin{array}{r}
1\times4+1\times2+1=\ 7 \\
1\times2+1=\ 3 \\
\hline
21
\end{array}
$$

$$1\times16+0\times8+1\times4+0\times2+1=\ 21$$

$$
\begin{array}{r}
10101 \\
\times\ 101 \\
\hline
10101 \\
00000 \\
10101 \\
\hline
1101001
\end{array}
\qquad
\begin{array}{r}
1\times16+0\times8+1\times4+0\times2+1=\ 21 \\
1\times4+0\times2+1=\ 5 \\
\hline
105
\end{array}
$$

$$1\times64+1\times32+0\times16+1\times8+0\times4+0\times2+1=105$$

15. $T(11)=66.$ $T(12)=78.$

16. $T(15)=\dfrac{15\times16}{2}=120.$ $T(20)=\dfrac{20\times21}{2}=210.$

$T(100)=\dfrac{100\times101}{2}=5050.$

17. $6^2=6\times6=36.$ $7^2=7\times7=49.$
     $10^2=10\times10=100.$ $13^2=13\times13=169.$

18. $T(14)+T(9)=150.$ $10^2+7^2+1^2=150.$

19. $6^3=6\times6\times6=216.$ $7^3=7\times7\times7=343.$
     $10^3=10\times10\times10=1000.$

20. The divisors of 28 that are less than 28 are 1, 2, 4, 7, and 14. $1+2+4+7+14=28.$

The divisors of 496 that are less than 496 are 1, 2, 4, 8, 16, 31, 62, 124, and 248. Their sum is 496.

The divisors of 8,128 that are less than 8,128 are 1, 2, 4, 8, 16, 32, 63, 127, 254, 508, 1,016, 2,032, and 4,064. Their sum is 8,128.

21. There are eight steps in dividing the milk. The drawings below show how much milk each pail contains after each step.

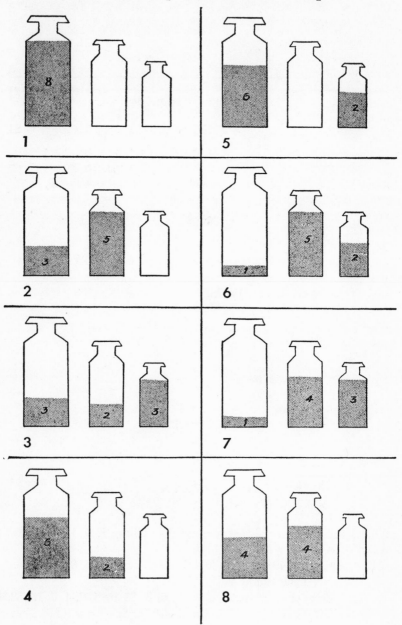

22.   Farmer Green brought back one of his own cows. This brought the total number of cows up to 18. He gave Tom one half of them, or 9 cows. He gave Dick one third of them, or 6 cows. He gave Harry one ninth of them, or 2 cows. His own cow was left, and he took it back.

23.   He divided the nine coins into three groups of three coins each. He took any two of these groups and weighed them against each other on the balance scale. If they balanced, then the third group contained the counterfeit coin. If they didn't balance, then the lighter group contained the counterfeit coin. In this way, one weighing picked out three coins, one of which was the counterfeit. Then he took any two of these three coins and weighed them against each other. If they balanced, then the third coin was counterfeit. If they did not balance, then the lighter one was the counterfeit.

24.   Abu's weights were 1, 2, 4, 8, and 16 pounds. To find out which weights to use to weigh out a certain number of pounds, he first wrote the number out in the two-scale. For example, the number, 17, when written in the two-scale, is 10,001, which means $1 \times 16 + 0 \times 8 + 0 \times 4 + 0 \times 2 + 1$. He used only those weights whose digits were equal to 1. So he would use the 16-pound weight and the 1-pound weight to weigh out 17 pounds.

Mustapha's weights were 1, 3, 9, and 27 pounds. The drawing below shows how the weights were placed to weigh out 7 pounds.

25.   The answer to this problem is the same no matter how long the hill is. To simplify the calculation let us say that the hill is 20 miles long. Then the round trip distance is 40 miles. Going uphill at 10 miles per hour takes 2 hours. Going downhill at 20 miles per hour takes 1 hour. So the total time for the round trip is 3 hours. Then the average speed for the round trip is $\dfrac{40 \text{ miles}}{3 \text{ hours}}$, or $13\frac{1}{3}$ miles per hour. You do *not* get the average speed by adding 10 and 20 and dividing by 2. To get an average speed you must divide the *total* distance by the *total* time.

26.   The answer to this problem is the same no matter how long the distance is. To simplify the calculation, let us say that the distance between New York and Chicago is 900 miles. Then the round trip distance is 1800 miles. If the average speed for the round trip is 60 miles per hour, then it takes 30 hours altogether. But if the 900 mile trip from New York to Chicago is made at a speed of 30 miles per hour, then it uses up the whole 30 hours, and there is no time left for the trip back. So the automobile would have to make the return trip in no time at all, and this, of course, is impossible.

27.   The circle on the face of the clock is divided into 60 equal parts. The minute hand travels around the circle at a speed of 60 spaces per hour. The hour hand follows it at a speed of 5 spaces per hour. So the minute hand gets ahead at a speed of 55 spaces per hour. The two hands will be together again when the minute hand is a full lap, or 60 spaces, ahead. To get that far ahead will take $^{60}\!/_{55}$ hours, which is $1\frac{1}{11}$ hours, or 1 hours and $5\frac{5}{11}$ minutes. So the hands will be together at $5\frac{5}{11}$ minutes past 1 o'clock.

28.   When the front end of the train enters the tunnel, the whole length of the train is still outside the tunnel. After the train travels one mile, the front end leaves the tunnel, but the whole length of the train is inside the tunnel. After it travels a second mile, the rear end of the train leaves the tunnel. So the time it takes to pass through is the time it takes to travel two miles. A speed of 15 miles per hour is a speed of 15 miles in 60 minutes, or 1 mile in 4 minutes. So it takes 8 minutes for the train to pass through the tunnel.

29.   To count the trains, let's take a ride on the train that leaves

120

New York at 9 A.M. Just as the train pulls out of the station, a train that left Philadelphia at 7 A.M. pulls in. This is the first train it meets. Just as the train pulls into the station in Philadelphia at 11 A.M., the 11 A.M. train pulls out. This is the last train it meets. So it meets the trains that left Philadelphia at 7 A.M., 8 A.M., 9 A.M., 10 A.M., and 11 A.M. It meets 5 trains altogether.

30. When Agamemnon makes his first trip, he travels faster than the bicycle he has just left. So he reaches the other bicycle first. This gives him time to fly back. When he flies back, again he gets there first, so there is time for another trip. In fact, after every trip there is time for another trip. So he makes an infinite number of trips, (more than any number there is). But, although he makes an indefinite number of trips, he travels a definite distance. The bicycles close the 250 mile gap between them at a speed of 25 miles per hour. So they meet in ten hours. In that time Agamemnon flies 20 × 10, or 200 miles.

31. She bought 1 pencil, 9 erasers, and 90 clips.

32. When the four pieces are put together to make the rectangle, they do not fit perfectly. There is a space in the middle of the rectangle that accounts for the extra square. It is barely noticed because it is spread out in a long and narrow parallelogram. In the drawing below, the parallelogram has been blackened to show where it is.

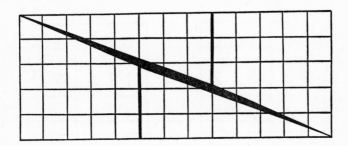

33. Mrs. Jones' apples are arranged below in groups of two. Each group is worth 1 cent. Beneath them, Mrs. Smith's apples are arranged in groups of three. Each of these groups is also worth 1 cent. If each group of three apples is combined with the group of two apples above it, we get 5 apples worth 2 cents. So there is no loss of money when these apples are sold at 5 for 2 cents. But after all the groups of three are used up, there are still five groups of twos left over. These five groups are worth 5 cents. But when the ten apples in these last groups are sold at 5 for 2 cents, they bring in only 4 cents. The penny was lost when these 10 apples were sold for less than they are worth.

34. Here are two arrangements for a 3 × 3 magic square. You can get others by writing the rows backward, or by writing the columns upside down.

8	1	6
3	5	7
4	9	2

6	7	2
1	5	9
8	3	4

35. To make a 5 × 5 magic square, follow these directions for placing the numbers from 1 to 25, putting them down in order: Place

the number 1 in the center box of the top row. Now move your pencil out of the box diagonally, through its upper right-hand corner. It will land outside the square. Move down to the opposite side, where you will place the number 2 in the bottom row. Now move diagonally up to the right again, and put the number 3 into the next box you enter. If you continue diagonally up to the right, your pencil lands outside once more. Cross over to the other side, and put the number 4 into the center box of the left-hand column. Now, again, go up diagonally to the right, and enter the number 5. This completes a group of five numbers. Go down one box to start the next group of five numbers. The 6 goes under the 5. Move up diagonally to the right, and place a number into each box you enter. If your pencil lands outside, move across to the opposite side. After each group of five numbers, go down one box to start the next group of five. When you finish the fifth group of five numbers, the number 25 will land in the center box of the bottom row.

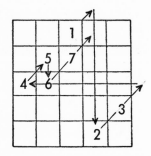

17	24	1	8	15
23	5	7	14	16
4	6	13	20	22
10	12	19	21	3
11	18	25	2	9

You can follow the same procedure to arrange the numbers from 1 to 49 in a 7×7 square, except that you enter the numbers in groups of seven, and go down one box after every seven numbers. To make a 9×9 square, go down one box after each group of nine numbers. This method can be used to make any magic square that has an odd number of boxes on a side.

36. First he took the lamb across, put it ashore, and then rowed back. Then he took the cabbage across, put it ashore, and took the lamb back with him. Then he took the wolf across, leaving the lamb behind. Then he returned alone to pick up the lamb.

37. The sleeping man was his son.

38. The wise man suggested that each should ride his brother's camel instead of his own. Then each could try to have his own camel arrive at Mecca last by doing his best to bring his brother's camel there first.

39. He fired the night watchman for sleeping on the job.

40. An electric train has no smoke.

41. Make the four cuts as shown in the drawing. The triangles cut from each arm of the cross will fit into the spaces between the arms.

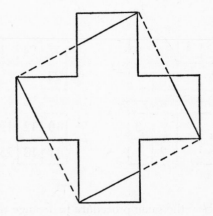

42. The first figure has two odd vertices. It can be done, if you start at one of the odd vertices. The second figure has no odd vertices. It can be done, starting at any vertex. The third figure has four odd vertices, so it cannot be done. The drawings below show how the two that can be done can be drawn without lifting the pencil, retracing any lines, or crossing any lines.

124

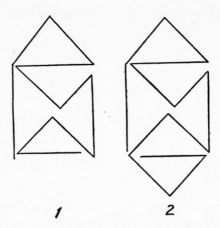

1   2

43. When you split the ring that has one twist, you get one big ring instead of two small ones. When you split the ring that has two twists, you get two rings that cannot be separated because they are linked together.

Index

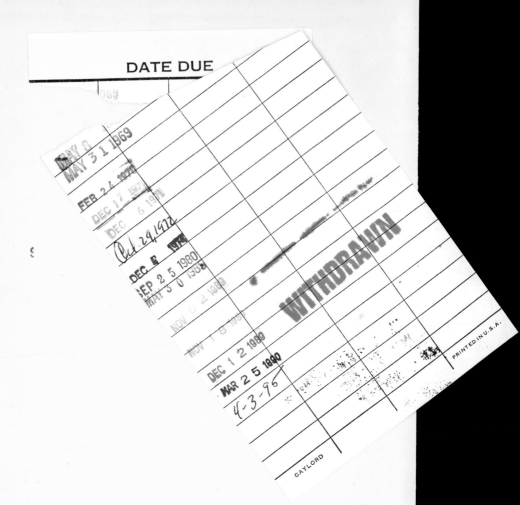